Albemarle County, Virginia Deed Book Abstracts

1794-1795

Ruth and Sam Sparacio

The Antient Press Collection
from

Colonial Roots
Millsboro, Delaware
2016

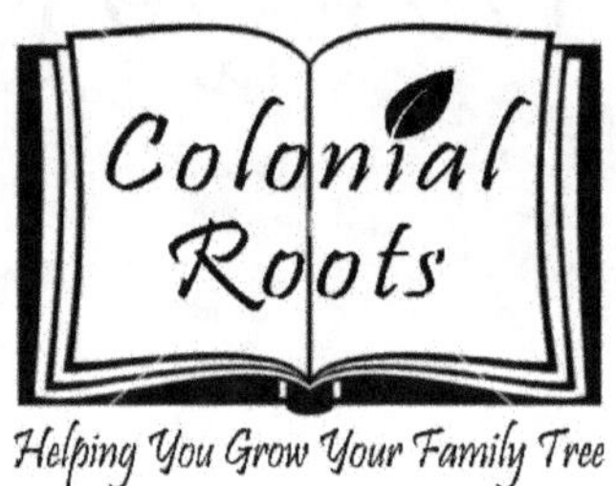

ISBN 978-1-68034-259-8

Originally printed 1999 by The Antient Press
Printed in the United States of America

CONTENTS

[this page intentionally blank]

ALBEMARLE COUNTY, VIRGINIA
DEED BOOK No. 11
1793-1795

pp. [On margin: KERR to BURCH, Deed]
258- THIS INDENTURE made the tenth day of July in the year of our Lord one
259 thousand seven hundred and ninety four; Between JAMES KERR of the County of Albemarle of the one part and SAMUEL BURCH of the same County of the other part; Witnesseth that JAMES KERR in consideration of the sum of eighty one pounds current money of Virginia to him in hand paid hath bargained and sold unto SAMUEL BURCH one certain parcel of land containing by estimation thirty six acres more or less lying in County of Albemarle and bounded; Begining at the Bridge on IVY CREEK, thence up the Creek as it meanders to SAMUEL BURCH's line, thence on the same North four degrees East one hundred twenty poles to the MOUNTAIN ROAD, thence down the same according to the different courses thereof to the first station; together with its appurtenances, To have and to hold the parcel of land with its appurtenances unto SAMUEL BURCH and his heirs and JAMES KERR doth covenant with SAMUEL BURCH and his heirs that the parcel of land with its appurtenances to SAMUEL BURCH his heirs will for ever warrant and defend, In Witness whereof JAMES KERR hath hereto set his hand and affixed his seal the day and year above written
Signed sealed and delivered in the presence of
[no witnesses recorded] JAMES KERR
At Albemarle July Court 1794
This Indenture was produced into Court and acknowledged by JAMES KERR, party thereto and ordered to be recorded
Teste JOHN NICHOLAS, C. A. C.

pp. [On margin: BATES's Wrt of ad quod damnum]
259- The Commonwealth of Virginia to the Sheriff of Albemarle County, Greeting;
260 You are hereby commanded to summon twelve good and lawful men of your Bailiwick as a Jury of Inquest opposite to the place where JOHN HARVIE formerly had a Mill on the fifth day of July next at the place where MOSES BATES proposes to abut the Dam of a Water Grist Mill which he hath petitioned our County Court for leave to erect, to view the lands proposed for the abutment, to locate and circumscribe by metes and bounds one acre belonging to RICHARD BURCH and to appraise the same according to its true value, to examine the lands above and below of the property of others which may be overflowed and say to what damages it will be of the several Proprietors and whether the Mansion House of any of the Proprietors or the Office or Garden thereunto immediately belonging or orchards will be overflowed, to inquire whether and in what degree fish of passage or ordinary navigation will be obstructed, whether by any and by what means such obstrction may be prevented and whether in their oinion the health of the neighbours will be annoyed by the stagnation of the waters and also all other the conveniences and inconveniences that may arise to individuals in consequence of erecting the said Mill which Inquest taken by virtue of this Writ signed and sealed by the Jurors return make to the

Justices of our County Court of Albemarle and have then and there this Writ, Witness JOHN NICHOLAS, Clerk of the Court of the County of Albemarle this twenty fifth day of June one thousand seven hundred and ninety four

JOHN NICHOLAS, C. A. C.

We the Jury being first sworn to secure a Writ of ad quod damnum issued from the worshipful Court of Albemarle in favour of MOSES BATES and hereto annexed did proceed to locate and lay off by metes and bounded one acre of land the property of RICHARD BURCH agreeable to a place hereto annexed, and do assess the sum of ten shillngs and proceeded to examine what lands of RICHARD BURCH that would be overflowed by the erecting a Mill at the place where JOHN HARVIE formerly had built a Mill and to be of the same height of water that the said HARVIE's Mill fomerly had and are of the opinion that the erecting of the said Mill Dam will overflow three acres of RICHARD BURCH's and so assess the damages for such overflowing to six pounds and the Jurors do further say that none of the inconveniences that are mentioned in the said Writ will be to any person and that no individual except RICHARD BURCH as aforesaid will be damaged and the Jurors do think that the building the said Mill will be of advantage to MOSES BATES and a conveniency to the neighbourhood.

GARLAND CARR	WILLIAM BUSTER	MENAN MILLS
JOSEPH GOODMAN	CLAUDIUS BUSTER	ISAAC MILLER
CHARLES GOODMAN	JESSE LEWIS	JOHN MICHIE
ROWLAND HORSLEY	HORSLEY GOODMAN	THOMAS BUSTER

[There is a drawing in the middle of the page for the acre of land, the one landmark being IVY CREEK]

The above is a true Plat of one acre of land directed to be laid off by the Court of Albemarle where MOSES BATES's Dam for a Water Grist Mill will abut on the land of RICHARD BURCH

ROBERT W. LEWIS

Executed in presents of RICHARD BURCH the return of the Jury and Surveyor's Plat.

JAMES KERR, Sheriff

At Albemarle July Court 1794

This Writ ad quod damnum with the Inquest of the Jury taken by vertue thereof together with the Plat of one acre of land condemned by the Jurors were returned to Court and ordered to be recorded

Teste JOHN NICHOLAS, C. A. C.

pp. {On margin: BROWN's Writ of ad quod damnum]
260- The Commonwealth of Virginia to the Sheriff of Albemarle County Greeting,
261 You are hereby commanded to summon twelve good and lawfull men of your Bailiwick to appear on the lands of JOSIAH WALLACE on MECHUMS RIVER between the WAGGON FORD and WALLACE's Barn on the eighth day of July next at the place where BENJAMIN BROWN proposed to abut the Dam of a Water Grist Mill which he petitioned our County Court for leave to erect to view the land proposed for the abutment, to locate and circumscribe by metes and bounds one acre belonging to JOSIAH WALLACE and to appraise the same according to its true value, to examine the lands above and below of the property of others which may

probably to overflow and say to what damage it will be of the several Proprietors and whether the Mansion House of any such Proprietor or the Offices or gardens thereunto immediately belonging or orchards will be overflowed , to inqure whether and in what degree fish of passage or ordinary navigation will be obstructed, whether by any and by what means such obstruction may be prevented, whether in their opinion the health of the Neighbours will be annoyed by the stagnation of the waters and also all other the conveniencies and inconveniencies that may arise to individuals in consequence of the Mill which Inquest so taken by virtue of this Writ signed and sealed by the Jurors due return make to the Justices of our County Court on the second Thursday in July next and have then and there this Writ; Witness JOHN NICHOLAS, Clerk of our said Court this twenty third day ofJune one thousand seven hundred and ninety four and in the eighteenth year of our Independence

JOHN NICHOLAS C. A. C.

In Obedience to a Writ of ad quod damnum from Albemarle Court directed us of the Jury to view he lands where the place at which the Dam is to cross MEACHUM's RIVER for the purpose of erecting a Water Grist Mll petitioned for by BENJAMIN BROWN and valued all damages which may accrue by overflowing up to the Fence of JOSIAH WALLACE and valued the land on the opposite side against which the Dam will be erected to ten shillings being first sworn according to Law [the right hand side of this entry is very faded, and only the folllowing Jurors can be read:]

WILLIAM GOOCH,	THOMAS BELL	JOHN ALPHIN
JOHN THOMAS	SAMUEL BURCH	NICHOLAS BURNLEY

In the center of the page is a Plat of the acre of land but too faded to make out any landmarks]

The above is a true plat of one acre of land directed to be laid off by the Court of Albemarle where BENJAMIN BROWN's Dam for aWater Grist Mill will abut on the land of JOSIAH WALLACE

ROBERT W. LEWIS

Executed the report of the Jury returned herewith together with the Plat

JAMES KERR, Sheriff

At Albemarle July Court 1794

This Writ of ad quid damnum with the Inquest of the Jury taken by vertue thereof together with the Plat of one acre of land condemned by the Jurors are returned into Court and ordered to be recorded

Teste JOHN NICHOLAS, C. A. C.

p. [On margin: CHARLOTTESVILLE Trustees to WARDLAW]

262 THIS INDENTURE made this seventeenth day of June one thousand seven hundred and ninety four; Between NICHOLAS LEWIS, THOMAS BELL, GEORGE DIVERS, CORNELIUS SCHENCK and ISAAC MILLER, a majority of the Trustees of the Town of CHARLOTTESVILLE in the County of Albemarle of one part and WILLIAM WARDLAW of the other part; Witnesseth that [the Trustees above named] by virtue and authority of a Trust reposed in them by an Act of the General Assembly of Virginia for that purpose made and provided, and also for and in consideratiion of the sum of thirty pounds current money of Virginia in hand paid by WILLIAM WARDLAW unto JOHN JOUETT, former Proprietor of the lands whereon sundry additional lotts are laid off and annexed to the Town of CHARLOTTESVILLE by vertue of the said Act of Assembly hath and by these presents doth bargain and sell unto WILLIAM WARDLAW one certain lott of land in the additional part of the

Town of CHARLOTTESVILLE containing by the Plat of the Town one half acre known by the number Fifty Nine in the Plan and Plat of the Town: To have and to hold the lott number fifty Nine to WILLIAM WARDLAW and his heirs and the [Trustees above named] do hereby warrant and for ever defend the lott of land unto WILLIAM WARDLAW against the claims of themselves jointly or severally or against the claims of their successors or heirs, In Witness whereof the [Trustees aforesaid] have set their hands and affixed their seals the day and year above written
Signed sealed and delivered in the presence of

[no witnesses recorded]

I acknowledge satisfaction for the said lott

JOHN JOUETT

At Albemarle July Court 1794
This Indenture was produced into Court and acknowledged by NICHOLAS LEWIS, THOMAS BELL, CORNELIUS SCHENCK and ISAAC MILLER, parties thereto, and ordered to be recorded

Teste JOHN NICHOLAS, C. A. C.

pp. [On margin: FERGUSON &c to BROADHEAD. Examined and delivered to A.
262- BROADHEAD]
263 THIS INDENTURE made this tenth day of July in the year of our Lord one thousand seven hundred and ninety four; Between LAWRENCE FERGUSON and DANIEL FERGUSON of one part and JONATHAN BROADHEAD of the other part, all of the County of Albemarle, Witnesseth that LAWRENCE FERGUSON and DANIEL FERGUSON for divers good causes and considerations but more especially in consideration of the sum of twenty two pounds current money of Virginia to them in hand paid, the receipt whereof they do hereby ackowledge do bargain and sell unto JONATHAN BROADHEAD his heirs one certain tract of land lying in County of Albemarle containing by estimation fifty acres be the same more or less and bounded by the lands of DANIEL FERGUSON on the North, by the lands of CHILES TERRELL on the West and by the lands of THOMAS EASTIN on the South which line joins the said FERGUSON, together with all its appurtenances; To have and to hold the tract of land with its appurtenances unto JONATHAN BROADHEAD his heirs and LAWRENCE FERGUSON and DANIEL FERGUSON for themselves and their heirs covenant with JONATHAN BROADHEAD and his heirs that the parcel of land with its appurtenances unto JONATHAN BROADHEAD and his heirs will warrant and forever defend against all persons whatsoever; InWitness whereof the said LAWRENCE and DANIEL hath hereunto set their hands and seals the day and year above written
Signed sealed and delivered in presence of

[no witnesses recorded]

LAWRENCE FERGUSON
DANIEL FERGUSON

At Albemarle July Court 1794
This Indenture was produced into Court and acknowledged by LAWRENCE FERGUSON and DANIEL FERGUSON, parties thereto, and ordered to be recorded

Teste JOHN NICHOLAS, C. A. C.

p. [On margin: BROOKS to PATTOn, Power of Attorney]
263 KNOW ALL MEN by these presents that I JAMES BROOKS of the County of AlBemarle do by these presents constitute and appoint Captain WILLIAM PATTON of MADISON County in the State of KENTUCKY my Attorney and I do hereby impower my Attorney to convey a tract of land containing four hundred and twenty acres lying in MADISON County in the said State of KENTUCKY which land I sold GEORGE CAMPBELL and I do also impower my said Attorney to grant in fee simple to the one half of a tract of land containing four hundred and twenty acres to GEORGE CAMPBELL to be joined in laying off the bounds for the land according to an Instrument of Writing given by me to GEORGE CAMPBELL and I do hereby further impower my Attoenry to do everything touching the premises as fully as I could myself. In Witness whereof I set my hand and seal this Ninth day of August 1794

JAMES BROOK

At Albemarle August court 1794
This Power of Attorney was produced into Court and acknowledged by JAMES BROOKS, party thereto, and ordered to be recorded
Teste JOHN NICHOLAS, C. A. C.

p. [On margin: JORDAN to HUGHES, Deed]
264 THIS INDENTURE made this twenty fourth day of July one thousand seven hundred and ninety two; Between FLEMING JORDAN of the State of GEORGIA by MATHEW JORDAN his Attorney by Power dated the seventh day of May one thousand seven hundred and ninety of the one part and WILLIAM HUGHES of the County of Albemarle of the other part; Witnesseth that FLEMING JORDAN by MATTHEW JORDAN his Attorney in consideration of the sum of forty pounds to him in hand paid by WILLIAM HUGHES, the receipt whereof he doth hereby acknowledge have bargained and sold unto WILLIAM HUGHES and his heirs a certain tract of land lying in County of Albemarle being part of a larger tract of land belonging to FLEMING JORDAN and which he inherits by the Last Will and Testament of his Father, MATHEW JORDAN, deceased, as divided and agreed by the other Legatees therein specified and adjoins the lands of WILLIAM HUGHES and known by the name of THE POCKET which is cut off from FLEMING JORDAN's tract by a line begining at a white Oak saplin on the River Bank and runing North thirty five degrees West with WILLIAM HUGHES's line as far as it goes and from thence the same course to the back line of FLEMING JORDAN and is supposed to contain thirty acres be the same more or less, To have and to hold the tract of land with the appurtenances thereunto belonging unto WILLIAM HUGHES and his heirs and FLEMING JORDAN by MATHEW JORDAN his Attorney for himself and his heirs the tract of land with the appurtenances to WILLIAM HUGHES his heirs will warrant anf for ever defend against himself and his heirs and against the claim of any other person; In Witness whereof FLEMING JORDAN by MATHEW JORDAN his Attorney hath hereunto set this hand and seal the day and date within written
Signed sealed and delivered in presence of

BENJAMIN JORDAN, FLEMING JORDAN
JOHN JORDAN, by MATHEW JORDAN
SAMUEL SHELTON, JUNR. his Attorney

OWEN LEWIS,
ROBERT HUGHES
At Albemarle September Court 1792
This Indenture was produced into Court and proved by the Oaths of SAMUEL SHELTON JUNR., and OWEN LEWIS, two of the witnesses thereto, And at Albemarle January Court 1794 was further proved by the Oath of ROBERT HUGHES, a third witness thereto, and ordered to be recorded
Teste JOHN NICHOLAS, C. A. C.

p. [On margin: RUCKER to GOODWIN, Deed]
265 THIS INDENTURE made this the twenty fourth day of March Anno Domini one thousand seven hundred and ninety four; Between REUBIN RUCKER of County of Albemarle of one part and THOMAS GOODWIN of Town of FREDERICKSBURG and County of SPOTSYLVANIA of the other part; Witnesseth that REUBIN RUCKER in consideration of sum of five shillings to him in hand paid by THOMAS GOODWIN the receipt whereof he doth hereby acknowledge, hath and by these presents doth bargain and sell unto THOMAS GOODWIN all that tract of land lying in Countys of Albemarle and ORANGE and which REUBIN RUCKER purchased of OLIVER TOWLES, together with the appurtenances thereof unto THOMAS GOODWIN and his heirs, But the true intent and meaning of these presents are such that REUBIN RUCKER and EDMUND FLYNT are indebted to THOMAS GOODWIN by Bond and open Account in the full and just sum of one hundred and sixty two pounds with Interest on one hundred and four pounds from the first day of December one thousand seven hundred and ninety two [the left side of the page is readable, the right side is not too faded] In Witness whereof REUBIN RUCKER hath hereunto set his hand and affixed his seal the day and year above written
Teste DANIEL GRINNAN REUBIN RUCKER
JOHN JONES
JAMES BLAIR
At Albemarle September Court 1794
This Indenture was produced into Court and acknowledged by REUBIN RUCKER, party thereto, and ordered to be recorded
Teste JOHN NICHOLAS, C. A. C.

pp. [On margin HUNTON's Executors to BELL, Deed]
266- THIS INDENTURE made this twenty second day of December one thousand
267 seven hundred and ninety three; Between ELIZABETH HUNTON, THOMAS WILLIAMS and ALEXANDER HUNTON, of RICHMOND County of one part and JOHN BELL of Albemarle County of the other part; Witnesseth that ELIZABETH HUNTON, THOMAS WILLIAMS and ALEXANDER HUNTON in consideration of two hundred and fifty five pounds current money of Virginia to them in hand paid the receipt whereof they do hereby acknowledge, hath and by these presents doth bargain and sell unto JOHN BELL his heirs one certain tract of land lying in County of Albemarle containing by estimation three hundred acres be the same more or less and bounded; Begining at a corner white Oak in THOMAS WALKER's line and runing thence a Southwesterly course by a line of marked trees to three large Chesnuts, thence continuing the same course to the Glebe Line making a corner to the

said land, from thence along the Glebe Line up the Mountain Northerly making a corner in HILL's line, thence along the Mountain and by the Grand Pattent to THOMAS WALKER's line making another corner, thence down the Mountain along a line of marked trees to the begining white Oak, including all the land above the line dividing between the Plantation that CHARLES B HUNTON now lives on and the parcels of land the same being three hundred acres more or less together with all water courses profits and advantages; To have and to hold the land and premises with their appurtenances unto JOHN BELL his heirs and ELIZABETH HUNTON, THOMAS WILLIAMS and ALEXANDER HUNTON doth further covenant and agree to and with JOHN BELL that they doth oblige themselves and their heirs to warrant and defend the right and title of the lands and premises unto JOHN BELL his heirs against the claim of every person, In Witness whereof ELIZABETH HUNTON, THOMAS WILLIAMS and ALEXANDER HUNTON hath hereunto set their hands and seals the day and year above written

Sealed and delivered in presence of

ROBERT HUNTON,	ELIZABETH her mark X HUNTON
NATHANIEL GORDON	THOMAS WILLIAMS
NATHANIEL WADDEL,	ALEXANDER HUTTON
JOHN GOODRIDGE, JUNR.	
WILLIAM BUCKNER, JUNR.	
WILLIAM RUCKER, JUNR.	

Received of JOHN BELL the day of the date of the within mentioned Deed, the sum of two hundred and fifty five pounds being the full consideration of the within bargained land and premises

Teste ROBERT HUNTON	ELIZABETH X HUNTON
NATHANIEL GORDON,	THOMAS WILLIAMS
JOHN GOODRIDGE, JUNR.	ALEXANDER HUNTON
WILLIAM BUCKNER, JUNR.	
WILLIAM RUCKER, JUNR.	

At Albemarle February Court 1794

The foregoing Indenture was produced into Court and proved by the Oath of NATHANIEL WADDEL, one of the witnesses thereto, And at July Court 1794, was further proved by the Oath of NATHANIEL GORDON, a second witness thereto, And at September Court 1794 was further proved by the Oath of JOHN GOODRIDGE, JUNR. and ordered to be recorded

Teste JOHN NICHOLAS, C. A. C.

pp. [On margin: LEWIS to MOON, Deed]
267- THIS INDENTURE made the seventh day of April one thousand seven hun-
268 dred and ninety four; Between JOHN LEWIS, SENR. of Albemarle County and RICHARD MOON of the said County of the other part; Witnesseth that JOHN LEWIS in consideration of the sum of twenty pounds current money in hand paid, the receipt whereof he doth hereby acknowledge hath bargained and sold unto RICHARD MOON and to his heirs one certain tract of land lying in County of Albemarle on the waters of HARDWARE RIVER known by the name of the MILL TRACT containing one hundred acres more or less bounded on the lands of [faded] MORRIS, WILLIAM MOON, SENR.and JOHN COLES together with all advan-

tages and appurtenances to the land and premises belonging; To have and to hold the tract of land with its appurtenances unto RICHARD MOON his heirs and JOHN LEWIS his heirs the land with its appurtenances unto RICHARD MOON and his heirs against the claim of any person shall warrant and defend by these presents; In Witness whereof JOHN LEWIS hath hereunto set his hand and seal the day and year above written

Signed sealed and delivered in presence of
WILLIAM HOPKINS, JOHN LEWIS
JACOB MOON,
RICHARDSON HAMNER

Memorandum: That on the day of the date of the within mentioned Indenture peaceable possession of the within mentioned land and premises was given to RICHARD MOON before the underwritten witnesses
Witness WILLIAM HOPKINS, JOHN LEWIS
JACOB MOON,
RICHARDSON HAMNER

April 7th 1794. Received of RICHARD MOON the sum of twenty pounds current money being the within mentioned consideration in full
Witness WILLIAM HOPKINS JOHN LEWIS
JACOB MOON,
RICHARDSON HAMNER

At Albemarle September Court 1794
The foregoing Indenture was produced into Court and proved by the Oaths of WILLIAM HOPKINS, JACOB MOON and RICHARDSON HAMNER, witnesses thereto, and ordered to be recorded
Tese JOHN NICHOLAS, C. A. C.

pp. [On margin: JAMISON to HOUK, Delivered to H. HOUK]
268- THIS INDENTURE made this eleventh day of September in the year of our
269 Lord one thousand seven hundred and ninety four Between SAMUEL JAMISON acting Executor of SAMUEL JAMISON, deceased, of the one part and HENRY HOUK each of the County of Albemarle of the other part; Witnesseth that in consideration of the sum of thirty pounds Virginia current money to him in hand paid, the receipt whereof SAMUEL JAMISON, Acting Executor, doth hereby acknowledge, hath pursuant to the Last Will and Testament of the deceased SAMUEL JAMISON hath and by these presents doth bargain and sell unto HENRY HOUK one certain tract of land containing by Pattent to said SAMUEL from BENJAMIN HARRISON Esqr. whilst Governor of Virginia, one hundred and fifty three acres lying in the County of Albemarle on some of the Branches of MOREMAN's RIVER and bounded, Begining at JOHN [Mc faded] to corner on a Pine runing thence along his lines South sixty two degrees East two hundred and sixty poles to pointers, North seventy one degrees East forty two poles to a Pine, thence a new line South twenty nine degrees East thirty seven poles to several saplins in JOHN RODES's line, thence along RODES's line South thirty seven degrees West fifteen poles to his corner Pine, new line South twenty four degrees West fifteen poles to BENJAMIN HUNTSMAN's corner pointer, thence along HUNTSMAN's ine North seventy eight degrees West one hundred and sixty three poles to a Pine, North sixty one degrees West forty

seven poles to pointers, West one hundred and twenty poles to a red Oak, thence new lines North sixty two degrees West thirty five poles to pointers, North eighteen degrees West thirty two poles to a Pine, North thirty six degrees East nineteen poles to JAMES WHERRY's corner white Oak,North twenty degrees East thirty two poles to pointers on the bank of MOREMAN's RIVER, thence down the River South sixty four and a half degrees West forty six poles crossing a Branch near its mouth to a Pine on a Hill, North thirty eight degrees East forty three poles to the begining; To have and to hold the land and premises with all the houses orchards and appurtenances thereunto belonging to HENRY HOUK and his heirs and SAMUEL JAMISON doth for himself and his heirs covenant with HENRY HOUK and his heirs that SAMUEL JAMISON will for ever warrant and defend the land with appurtenances to HENRY HOUK and his heirs against the claim of every person; In Witness whereof SAMUEL JAMISON hath hereunto set his hand and affixed his seal the day and year above written
Signed sealed and delivered in presence of
[no witnesses recorded] SAMUEL JAMISON
At Albemarle September Court 1794
The foregoing Indenture was produced into Court and acknowledged by SAMUEL JAMISON, party thereto, and ordered to be recorded
Teste JOHN NICHOLAS C. A. C.

pp. [On Margin; GENTRY to TAYLOR
269- THIS INDENTURE made this second day of September one thousand seven
270 hundred and ninety four; Between BARTELOTT GENTRY of Albemarle
County of one part and WOULDRY TAYLOR of the same County of the other part; Witnesseth that BARTELOTT GENTRY in consideration of the sum of one hundred pounds to him in hand paid, the receipt whereof I do hereby acknowledge, hath and by these presents doth bargain and sell unto WOULDRY TAYLOR to him and his heirs a certain tract of land being in County of Albemarle, Begining [faded] near NICHOLAS BURNLEY runing thence [faded] near the Old Field, thence [faded] GEORGE WILLIAMS's Spring Branch thence down the Branch [faded] line to a certain Poplar, thence leaving the [faded] line to a small white Oak standing in the Glade, thence [faded] corner white Oak standing on said Branch, [faded] MILLS's Old Line to a corner called NICHOLAS BURNLEY, thence on his line to the begining; To have and to hold the tract of land with the appurtenances to WOULDRY TAYLOR and his heirs without any hindrance from BARTELOTT GENTRY or his heirs, And BARTELOTT GENTRY for himself and his heirs the land and premises with the appurtnances unto WOULDRY TAYLOR his heirs will warrant and forever defend against the claim of every person; In Witness whereof BARTELOTT GENTRY hath hereunto set his hand and seal the day and year first above written
Signed sealed and delivered in the presence of
DANIEL MAUPIN, JUNR. BARTLETT GENTRY
BENNETT GILLUM
JOHN MAUPIN
WILLIAM GOODING
At Albemarle September Court 1794
The foregoing Indenture was presented in Court and proved by the Oaths of

DANIEL MAUPIN, JUNR., BENNETT GILLUM and JOHN MAUPIN, three of the witnesses thereto, and ordered to be recorded
Teste JOHN NICHOLAS, C. A. C.

pp. [On margin: KENNERLY to HARRIS, Deed]
270- THIS INDENTURE made this twentyeth day of March one thousand seven
271 hundred and ninety four; Between THOMAS KENNERLY of GEORGIA of one part and THOMAS HARRIS of Albemarle County of the other part; Witnesseth that THOMAS KENNERLY hath in consideration of the sum of fifty pounds current money of Virginia to him in hand paid by THOMAS HARRIS, the receipt whereof THOMAS KENNERLY doth hereby acknowledge, hath and by these presents doth bargain and sell unto THOMAS HARRIS his heirs one certain tract of land containing by estimation fifty acres be the same more or less lying in County of Albemarle and bounded, Begining at a Dogwood side line in JAMES HARRIS's and THOMAS KENNERLY's Old Line, runing thence South sixteen degrees West seventy poles to corner pointers on the top of a ridge, thence South forty eight degrees West ninety six poles to pointers, thence North ten degrees East twelve poles to a Dogwood at the corner of WILLIAM MAUPIN's Fence DOGWOOD BOTTOM or BUDDING TREE HILL thence North fifty two degrees East one hundred and ninety four poles to the begining; To have and to hold the tract of land with all and singular the appurtenances thereunto belonging unto THOMAS HARRIS his heirs, and THOMAS KENNERLY for himself and his heirs doth covenant with THOMAS HARRIS that he will warrant and defend the tract of land with appurtenances unto THOMAS HARRIS his heirs free from the claim of all persons, In Witness whereof I THOMAS KENNERLY have hereunto set my hand and affixed my seal the day and year first above written
Signed sealed and delivered in the presenceof
JAMES HARRIS THOMAS KENNERLY
NATHAN HARRIS
ANNE HARRIS
JAMES HARRISON

Memo: that on the day and year within written peaceable and quiet possession was had and taken by THOMAS KENNERLY and by him given to THOMAS HARRIS his heirs and assigns
Teste JAMES HARRIS THOMAS KENNERLY
NATHAN HARRIS
ANNE HARRIS
JAMES HARRISON

26th of March 1794. Received the full consideration money in this Deed expressed, received by me
Teste JAMES HARRIS, THOMAS KENNERLY
NATHAN HARRIS,
ANNE HARRIS,
JAMES HARRISON

At Albemarle September Court 1794
The foregoing Indenture was produced into Court and proved by the Oaths of JAMES HARRIS, NATHAN HARRIS and JAMES HARRISON, three of the witnesses thereto, and ordered to be recorded Teste JOHN NICHOLAS, C. A. C.

p. [On margin: MELTON's Trustees to SUTTON, Deed]
271 THIS INDENTURE made this seventeenth day of May in the year of our Lord one thousand seven hundred and ninety four, Between CHARLES L. LEWIS, WILLIAM CLARK, EDWARD MOORE and HOWEL LEWIS, a majority of the Trustees for the Town of MELTON by Act of Assembly of the one part and WILLIAM SUTTON of the County of Albemarle of the other part; Witnesseth that CHARLES L. LEWIS, WILLIAM CLARK, EDWARD MOORE and HOWEL LEWIS by vertue of an Act of Assembly for establishing the Town of MELTON on the lands of BENNETT HENDERSON in the County of Albemarle and for and in consideratiion of the sum of fifteen pounds current money of Virginia to them in hand paid by WILLIAM SUTTON the receipt whereof they do hereby acknowledge, hath and by these presents doth bargain and sell unto WILLIAM SUTTON one certain lott of land containing half an acre in the Plat of the Town number Fifteen, To have and to hold with all and singular the appurtenances thereunto belonging unto WILLIAM SUTTON and to his heirs and the Trustees aforesaid the lott of ground unto WILLIAM SUTTON and to his heirs will warrant and forever defend by these presents; In Witness whereof the Trustees aforesaid have hereunto set their hands and affixed their seals the day and year first above written

Signed sealed and delivered in the presence of

F. TALIAFERRO	CHARLES L. LEWIS
T. WOODSON	WILLIAM CLARK
BENNETT HENDERSON	EDWARD MOORE
	HOWEL LEWIS

At Albemarle September Court 1794

The foregoing Indenture was produced into Court and proved by the Oaths of FRANCIS TALIAFERRO, TARLTON WOODSON and BENNETT HENDERSON, witnesses thereto, and ordered to be recorded

Teste JOHN NICHOLAS, C. A. C.

pp. [On margin: MELTON's Trustees to SHIFLETT, Deed]
271- THIS INDENTURE made this 14th day of July one thousand seven hundred
272 and ninety four; Between EDWARD MOORE, CHARLES L. LEWIS, WILLIAM CLARK and HOWEL LEWIS a majority of the Trustees for the Town of MELTON by Act of Assembly of one part and JOEL SHIFLETT of County of Albemarle of the other part; Witnesseth that EDWARD MOORE, CHARLES L. LEWIS, WILLIAM CLARK and HOWEL LEWIS by virtue of an Act of Assembly for establishing the Town aforesaid on the lands of BENNETT HENDERSON in the County of Albemarle and in consideration of the sum of twenty eight pounds current money of Virginia to them in hand paid by JOEL SHIFLETT, the receipt whereof they do hereby acknowledge, hath bargained and sold unto JOEL SHIFLETT and to his heirs a lott of land containing one half acre and marked in the plan of the Town number [26], To have and to hold the lott of ground with all and singular the appurtenances thereunto belonging unto JOEL SHIFLETT and his heirs and the Trustees aforesaid do hereby covenant that the lott of land with all appurtenances unto JOEL SHIFLETT his heirs against the claim of all persons will warrant and by these presents for ever defend, In Witness whereof the Trustees aforesaid have hereunto set their hands and affixed their seals the day and year first above written

Signed sealed and delivered in the presence of

RICHARD BARBOUR,	EDWARD MOORE
JOHN THOMAS	CHARLES L. LEWIS
WILLIAM D. MERIWETHER	WILLIAM CLARK
BENNETT HENDERSON	HOWELL LEWIS

At Albemarle September Court 1794
The foregoing Indenture was produced into Court and acknowledged by EDWARD MOORE, CHARLES L. LEWIS, WILLIAM CLARK and HOWELL LEWIS, parties thereto, and ordered to be recorded
Teste JOHN NICHOLAS, C. A. C.

pp. [On margin: MELTON's Trustees to BUTLER, Deed]
272- THIS INDENTURE made this 14th day of July in the year of our Lord one
273 thousand seven hundred and ninety four; Between EDWARD MOORE, CHARLES L. LEWIS, WILLIAM CLARK and HOWELL LEWIS, a majority of the Trustees for the Town of MELTON by Act of Assembly of one part and EDWARD BUTLER of the County of Albemarle of the other part; Witnesseth that EDWARD MOORE, CHARLES L. LEWIS, WILLIAM CLARK and HOWELL LEWIS by virtue of an Act of Assembly for establishing the Town of MELTON on the lands of BENNETT HENDERSON in the County of Albemarle in consideration of the sum of thirteen pound, fifteen shillings current money of Virginia to them in hand paid by EDWARD BUTLER, the receipt whereof they do hereby acknowledge have bargained and sold unto EDWARD BUTLER and to his heirs one certain parcel of land containing half an acre and marked in the plan of the Town number [5] To have and to hold the lott of ground with appurtenances thereunto belonging unto EDWARD BUTLER his heirs and the Trustees aforesaid doth covenant that the lott of ground with all appurtenances theretunto belonging unto EDWARD BUTLER his heirs against the claim of every person whatsoever will warrant and by these presents defend, In Witness whereof EDWARD MOORE, CHARLES L. LEWIS, WILLIAM CLARK and HOWELL LEWIS hath hereunto set their hands and affixed their seals the day and year first above written
Signed sealed and delivered in the presence of

RICHARD BARBOUR,	EDWARD MOORE
JOHN THOMAS,	CHARLES L. LEWIS
WILLIAM D. MERIWETHER	WILLIAM CLARK
BENNETT HENDERSON	HOWELL LEWIS

At Albemarle September Court 1794
The foregoing Indenture was produced into Court and acknowledged by EDWARD MOORE, CHARLES L. LEWIS, WILLIAM CLARK and HOWELL LEWIS, parties thereto, and ordered to be recorded
Teste JOHN NICHOLAS, C. A. C.

pp. [On margin; MELTON's Trustees to SNELSON, Deed]
273- THIS INDENTURE made this 17th day of May in the year of our Lord one
274 thousand seven hundred and ninety four; Between WILSON CARY NICHOLAS, EDWARD MOORE, CHARLES LILBURN LEWIS, WILLIAM CLARK and HOWELL LEWIS, a majorty of the Trustees of the Town of MELTON

established by Act of Assembly in the year one thousand seven hundred and eighty nine of the one part and ROBERT SNELSON of County of Albemarle of the other part; Witnesseth that the Trustees aforesaid by virtue of the power vested in them by the Act of Assembly for the establishment of the Town aforesaid on the lands of BENNETT HENDERSON in the County of Albemarle and in consideration of the sum of twelve pounds to them in hand paid by ROBERT SNELSON, the receipt whereof they do hereby acknowledge, have bargained and sold unto ROBERT SNELSON and his heirs a certain lot of land containing half an acre and in the Plan of the Town number [28], To have and to hold the lott of land with all and singular the appurtenances thereunto belonging to ROBERT SNELSON and his heirs and the Trustees aforesaid doth covenant and agree that the parcel of land with appurtenances unto ROBERT SNELSON his heirs will warrant and forever defend, In Witness whereof WILSON, EDWARD, CHARLES, WILLIAM and HOWELL have hereunto set their hands and affixed their seals the day and year first above written

In presence of

Teste RICHARD PRICE, CHARLES L. .LEWIS
PETER MARTIN, WILLIAM CLARK
ELISHA D. GILLUM EDWARD MOORE
JOHN HENDERSON HOWELL LEWIS

At Albemarle September Court 1794

The foregoing Indenture was produced into Court and acknowledged by CHARLES L. LEWIS, WILLIAM CLARK, EDWARD MOORE and HOWELL LEWIS, Witnesses thereto, and ordered to be recorded

Teste JOHN NICHOLAS C. A. C.

p. [On margin: MELTON's Trustees to GAMBILL, Deed]
274 THIS INDENTURE made tjos 11th day of April in the year of our Lord one thousand seven hundred and ninety four; Between WILSON CARY NICHO LAS, CHARLES LILBURN LEWIS, WILLIAM CLARK and HOWELL LEWIS a majority of the Trustees of the Town of MELTON established by an Act of Assembly in the year one thousand seven hundred and eighty nine of the one part and JOHN GAMBILL of County of Albemarle of the other part; Witnesseth that the Trustees aforesaid by virtue of the said recited Act for the establishment of the Town of MELTON on the lands o BENNETT HENDERSON in the County of Albemarle and in consideration of the sum of sixteen pounds current money of Virginia to them in hand paid by JOHN GAMBILL, the receipt wehreof they do hereby acknowledge, have bargained and sold unto JOHN GAMBILL and his heirs a certain lott of land containing one half acre and marked in theplan of the Town number [12], To have and to hold the lott of land with all appurtenances thereunto belonging unto JOHN GAMBILL and his heirs and he Trustees aforesaid do hereby covenant and agree that the parcel of land with all its appurtenanes for themselves and their heirs against the claim of all persons shall warrant and forever defend, InWitness whereof WILSON CARY NICHOLAS, EDWARD MOORE, CHARLES L. LEWIS, WILLIAM CLARK and HOWELL LEWIS hath hereunto set their hands and affixed their seals the day and year first above written

In presence of MENAN MILLS WILSON CARY NICHOLAS
R. GARLAND CHARLES L. LEWIS

RICHARD PRICE

EDWARD MOORE
WILLIAM CLARK
HOWELL LEWIS

At Albemarle September Cour 1794
The foregoing Indenture was produced into Court and acknowledgedby WILSON CARY NICHOLAS, CHARLES L. LEWIS, EDWARD MOORE WILLIAM CLARK and HOWELL LEWIS, parties thereto, and ordered to be recorded
Teste JOHN NICHOLAS, C. A. C.

pp, [On margin: BROWN to SOILAR, Deed]
274- THIS INDENTURE made the 8th day of September in the year of our Lord
275 one thousand seven hundred and ninety four; Between JOHN BROWN and MARY his Wife of County of Albemarle of one part and HENRY SOILAR of County of Albemarle of other part; Witnesseth that JOHN BROWN in consideration of sum of twenty six pounds current money of Virginia to him in haid paid by HENRY SOILAR, the receipt whereof he doth hereby acknowledge, hath bargained and sold unto HENRY SOILAR and his heirs one certain tract of land lying in County of Albemarle on BEVER CREEK containing fifty two acres and bounded; Begining at a red Oak on the side of the Road just above WILLIAM BAILEY's thence runing North eighty degrees West eighty two poles to a white Oak and Hiccory, thence North fifty degrees West nineteen poles to the Road, thence South forty degrees West cornering with the differenct courses of the Road one hundred and forty one poles to a corner shingle stump, thence due East down the Road ninety nine poles to the begining; To have and to hold the tract of land with all and singular the appurtenances thereunto belonging unto HENRY SOILAR his heirs free from the claim of any person, In Witness whereof JOHN BROWN and MARY his Wife have hereunto set their hands and seals the day and year first above written
Signed sealed and delivered in presence of

BENJAMIN PORTER, JOHN BROWN
ATHANASUS THOMAS, MARY BROWN
ELIJAH GARTH,
BERNIS BROWN

Memorandum: that on the day and year within mentioned quiet and peaceable possession and seizin was had and taken by the parties within mentioned according to the true purport of the meaning of the within mentioned Indenture as witness my hand and seal the date within mentioned

Teste BENJAMIN PORTER, JOHN BROWN
ATHANASUS THOMAS,
ELIJAH GARTH
BERNIS BROWN

Received this 8th day of September 1794 of Mr. HENRY SOYLER twenty six pounds, it being the consideration money of this within mentioned Deed

Teste BENJAMIN PORTER JOHN BROWN
ATHANASUS THOMAS

At Albemarle September Court 1794
The foregoing Indenture was produced into Court and ackowledged by JOHN BROWN party thereto, and ordered to be recorded Teste JOHN NICHOLAS, C. A. C.

pp. [On margin: RODES to HARRIS, Deed]
275- THIS INDENTURE made this 12th day of September one thousand seven
276 hundred and ninety three: Between CLIFTON RODES, formerly Sheriff of Albemarle County of one part and JOEL HARRIS of the same County of the other part; Witnesseth that CLIFTON RODES, Sheriff, hath sold agreeable to the clauses in the Revenue Act of Assembly a certain tract of land formerly the property of JAMES DUFFEY lying on both sides MOREMAN's RIVER and adjoining the foot of the PASTURE FENCE MOUNTAIN in the County aforesaid and sold for ninety acres made this twelfth day of September 1793, Begining at the said JOEL HARRIS's pointers, thence new lines North forty four degrees West fifty nine poles to a Chesnut Oak, thence North twenty seven degrees East forty one poles to a Hiccory, thence North fourteen degrees West sixty three poles to a Hiccory, thence South thirty three degrees West one hundred and forty eight poles to pointers on AGNESS McCORD's line, South forty six and an half degrees East sixty poles crossing the River to a corner, thence South ten and an half degrees East twenty poles to a Spanish Oak, thence new lines seventy degees East eighty two poles to pointers on JOEL HARRIS's line, thence on his line North five degrees West seventy two poles crossing the River to the begining, and in consideration of the sum of seven shillings and three pence three farthings specie and three shillings and eleven pence Certificate to him in hand paid by JOEL HARRIS for the Revenue for which the Act was provided and by these presents CLIFTON RODES do make over and confirm to JOEL HARRIS his heirs; In Witness whereof CLIFTON RODES, Sheriff, hath hereunto set his hand and seal this day and date above mentioned

Teste F. TALIAFERRO, CLIFTON RODES
ISHAM WATKINS
JOHN RODES
DAVID KERR

At Albemarle September Court 1793
The foreging Indenture ws produced into Court and proved by the Oaths of FRANCIS TALIAFERRO and JOHN RODES, two of the witnesseth thereto, And at September Court 1794 was further proved by the Oath of DAVID KERR, a third witness thereto, and ordered to be recorded

Teste JOHN NICHOLAS, C. A. C.

pp. [On margin: WINSTON to HARRIS, Deed. Examined and delivered to JOEL
276- HARRIS 2d of October 1825].
277 THIS INDENTURE made this fourth day of January one thousand seven hundred and ninety four; Between WILLIAM OVERTON WINSTON of the County of HANOVER of one part and THOMAS HARRIS and JOEL HARRIS of Albemarle County of the other part; Witnesseth that WILLIAM O. WINSTON in consideration of sum of one hundred pounds current money of Virginia to him in hand paid by THOMAS and JOEL HARRIS, the receipt whereof he doth hereby acknowledge, hath and by these presents doth bargain and sell unto THOMAS and JOEL HARRIS and their heirs one certain tract of land containing one hundred and fifty acres more or less lying in County of Albemarle on an arm of the GREAT MOUNTAINS and bounded; Begining at BENJAMIN BROWN, SENIOR his corner at Chesnuts and Chesnut Oak saplins runing thence North fifty one degrees West thirty

four poles to a corner Chesnut red Oak, North seven degrees East sixty eight poles to a corner white Oak, North fifty four degrees East forty poles to a corner Hiccory, North two degrees East seventy four poles to two corner Chesnut red Oaks, North thirty one degrees East forty eight poles to a corner Chesnut, North fifty degrees East seventy four poles to a corner white Oak, South seven degrees East eighty poles to a corner white Oak, South forty degrees West one hundred and sixteen poles to a corner red Oak, South fifty degrees East forty two poles to a corner Hiccory, South twenty degrees West one hundred and thirty two poles to a corner Chesnut red Oak in BENJAMIN BROWN, SENIOR's lne, thence on his line North forty three degrees West forty four poles to a corner Chesnut, thence South eighty degrees West twenty poles to the begining; To have and to hold the tract of land with its appurtenances unto THOMAS and JOEL HARRIS and to their heirs without the hindrance of WILLIAM O. WINSTON or any other person claiming under him and WILLIAM O. WINSTON for himself and his heirs the tract of land unto THOMAS and JOEL HARRIS and their heirs will warrant and forever defend by these presents; in Witness whereof WILLIAM O. WINSTON hath hereunto set his hand and affixed his seal the day and date first above written

Signed sealed and delivered in presence of
BERNARD BROWN — WILLIAM O. WINSTON
CHARLES B. HUNTON,
T. DIVERS

Memorandum: That on the day and year within written quiet and peaceable possession was had and taken by the within parties according to the true meaning of this Indenture, Witness my hand the day and year first above written

In presence of BERNARD BROWN, — WILLIAM O. WINSTON
CHARLES B. HUNTON
T. DIVERS

Received of the within named THOMAS and JOEL HARRIS the consideration money expressed in the within Deed in full, received by me

Teste BERNARD BROWN, — WILLIAM O. WINSTON
CHARLES B. HUNTON,
T. DIVERS

At Albemarle June Court 1794

The foregoing Indenture was produced into Court and proved by the Oaths of BERNARD BROWN and THOMAS DIVERS, two of the witnesses thereto, and at September Court 1794, was further proved by the Oath of CHARLES B. HUNTON, a third witness thereto, and ordered to be recorded

Teste JOHN NICHOLAS, C. A. C.

pp. [On margin: KENNERLY to HARRIS, Deed]
277- THIS INDENTURE made this third day of April Anno Domini one thousand
278 seven hundred and ninety four; Between THOMAS KENNERLY of the State of GEORGIA of one part and NATHAN HARRIS of Albemarle County of the other part; Witnesseth that THOMAS KENNERLY in consideration of the sum of twenty four pounds current money of Virginia to him in hand paid by NATHAN HARRIS, the receipt whereof THOMAS KENNERLY doth hereby acknowledge, hath and by these presents doth bargain and sell unto NATHAN HARRIS and to his heirs

a certain tract of land by estimation two hundred and twenty six acres be the same more or less lying in County of Albemarle at the foot of the GREAT MOUNTAINS BROWN's COVE and bounded, joining the lands of THOMAS HARRIS, WILLIAM MAUPIN, JOHN HARVIE and the said NATHAN HARRIS being the land deeded from JOHN BRICE to THOMAS KENNERLY, To have and to hold the tract of land with all its appurtenances thereunto belonging unto NATHAN HARRIS and to his heirs without the hindrance of THOMAS KENNERLY his heirs and THOMAS KENNERLY and his heirs will warrant and forever defend the tract of land against all persons. In Witness whereof THOMAS KENNERLY hath hereunto set his hand and affixed his seal the day and date first above written

Signed sealed and delivered in presence of

JAMES HARRIS, THOMAS KENNERLY
ROBERT TURNER,
ROBERT BROWN,
BERNARD BROWN

Memorandum, That on the third day of April one thousand seven hundred and ninety four quiett and peaceable possession and seizin of the land and premises within mentioned in this Deed was by THOMAS KENNERLY delivered to NATHAN HARRIS according to the form and effect of this Deed

In presence of JAMES HARRIS, THOMAS KENNERLY
ROBERT TURNER
ROBERT BROWN
BERNARD BROWN

3d of April. Received of the within named NATHAN HARRIS the full consideration money in this Deed expressed, I say received by me

Teste JAMES HARRIS, THOMAS KENNERLY
ROBERT TURNER
ROBERT BROWN
BERNARD BROWN

At Albemarle September Court 1794

The foregoing Indenture was produced into Court and proved by the Oaths of JAMES HARRIS, ROBERT BROWN and BERNARD BROWN, three of the witnesses thereto and ordered to be recorded

Teste JOHN NICHOLAS, C. A. C.

p. [On margin: BERRY to MULLINS, Deed]

279 THIS INDENTURE made this eighth day of March in the year of our Lord one thousand seven hundred and seventy nine; Between BENJAMIN BERRY of ORANGE County of one part and JOHN MULLINS of Albemarle County of other part; Witnesseth that in consideration of sum of thirty five pounds current money of Virginia to BENJAMIN BERRY in hand paid and himself therewith fully satisfied the receipt whereof he doth hereby acknowledge, hath bargained and sold one certain tract of land situate in County of Albemarle on both sides of the North Fork of a Branch of BEVER CREEK containing one hundred and eighty one acres be the same more or less and bounded; Begining at a corner Stake runing thence North sixteen degrees East nineteen poles, thence North sixty six degrees East ninety poles, North ten degrees West eighty poles, North seventy five degrees West one hundred twenty

two poles, South seventy three degrees West one hundred twenty two poles, South ten degrees West seventy nine poles, South seventy degrees West one hundred seventy eight poles to the begining, with all houses and all and every of the appurtenaces thereunto belonging; To have and to hold the tract of land with appurtenances unto JOHN MULLINS and his heirs and BENJAMIN BERRY for himself and his heirs the tract of land unto JOHN MULLINS his heirs against the claim and demand of any person will warrant and forever defend by these presents; In Witness whereof BENJAMIN BERRY hath interchangeably set his hand and affixed his seal the day and year first above written
Signed sealed and delivered in presence of us
MATHEW MULLINS BENJAMIN BERRY
JEREMIAH YANCEY,
ROBERT HARRIS
[There is no recording recorded at the end of this Indenture.]

pp. [On margin; BERRY to MULLINS, Deed]
279- THIS INDENTURE made this eighth day of March in the year of our Lord one
280 thousand seven hundred and seventy nine, Between BENJAMIN BERRY of ORANGE County of the one part and JOHN MULLINS of County of Albemarle of the other part; Witnesseth that in consideration of the sum of thirty five pounds current money of Virginia to BENJAMIN BERRY in hand paid and himself therewith fully satisfied the receipt whereof he doth hereby acknowledge, hath bargarined and sold unto JOHN MULLINS one certain tract of land sitaute in County of Albemarle on both sides of the North Fork of a Branch of BEVER CREEK containing one hundred and eighty one acres be the same more or less and bounded, Begining at a corner Stake and runing thence North sixteen degrees East nineteen poles, thence North sixty six degrees East ninety poles, North ten degrees West eighty poles, North seventy five degrees West one hundred and twenty tw poles, South seventy three degrees West one hundred and twenty two poles, South ten degrees West seventy nine poles, South seventy degrees West one hundred seven eight poles to the begining with all houses orchards and appurtenances thereunto belonging, To have and to hold the land and premises unto JOHN MULLINS his heirs and BENJAMIN BERRY for himself and his heirs the land and premises with the appurtenances unto JOHN MULLINS his heirs against the claim of every person will warrant end forever defend by these presents; In Witness whereof BENJAMIN BERRY hath interchangeably set his hand and affixed his seal the day and year first above written
Signed sealed and delivered in presence of
MATHEW MULLINS, BENJAMIN BERRY
JEREMIAH YANCEY
ROBERT HARRIS,
BARTELOTT GENTRY A Copy
JOHN MAUPIN, Teste JOHN NICHOLAS, C.A..C
ROBERT JONES
At Albemarle September Court 1779
The foregoing Indenture was produced into Court and proved by the Oaths of MATHEW MULLINS and JEREMIAH YANCEY, two of the witnesses thereto, and at September Court 1794, an attested copy of this Indenture was produced into Court and an acknowledgment of it being a true copy from this Indenture proved by

the Oaths of JOHN MAUPIN, one of the subscribing witnesses thereto, which copy together with the Original were ordered to be recorded
Test JOHN NICHOLAS, C. A. C.

pp. [On margin; SHELTON to WOODSON, Deed]
280- THIS INDENTURE made this eighth day of September in the year of our Lord
281 one thousand seven hundred and ninety four; Between THOMAS SHELTON
of the County of Albemarle of the one part and TARLTON WOODSON of the same County of the other part; Witnesseth that THOMAS SHELTON and MARY his Wife and ELIZABETH his Mother in consideration of the sum of one hundred pounds current money of Virginia in hand paid to THOMAS SHELTON and MARY his Wife and ELIZABETH his Mother, the receipt whereof we do hereby acknowledge, have bargained and sold unto TARLTON WOODSON one certain tract of land containing ninety six acres be the same more or less lying in the aforesaid County and on MECHUM's RIVER and bounded by the lands of WILLIAM [BE] WILLIAM JARMAN, JESSE TORREY and BENJAMIN TAYLOR's lines and so including the Plantation whereon THOMAS SHELTON now lives which lands THOMAS SHELTON and MARY his Wife and ELIZABETH his Mother doth convey unto TARLTON WOODSON with all houses and appurtenances thereunto belonging, To have and to hold the land and premises with the appurtenances unto TARLTON WOODSON and his heirs and THOMAS SHELTON and MARY his Wife and ELIZABETH his Mother do by these presents for themselves and their heirs covenant that they will for ever warrant and defend the land and premises with the appurtenances unto TARLTON WOODSON his heirs by these presents; In Witness whereof we have hereunto set our hands and seals the day and year first above written
Signed sealed and delivered in presence of

CHARLES BAILEY, THOMAS his mark X SHELTON
WILLIAM PERKINS, MARY SHELTON
CHARLES BAILEY, ELIZABETH her mark X SHELTON
JESSE TORREY

Received the day and date of the within mentioned Deed of the within named TARLTON WOODSON the sum of one hundred pounds current money of Virginia, it being the full consideration of the within mentioned land and temement

Teste JESSE TORREY THOMAS his mark X SHELTON
CHARLES BAILEY, MARY SHELTON
WILLIAM PERKINS, ELIZABETH her mark X SHELTON
CHARLES BAILEY

At Albemarle September Court 1794
The foregong Indenture was produced into Court and acknowledged by THOMAS SHELTON and MARY his Wife, she being first privily examined as the Law directs, and proved as to ELIZABETH SHELTON by the Oaths of CHARLES BAILEY, JESSE TORREY and WILLIAM PERKINS, three of the witnesses thereto. and ordered to be recorded Teste JOHN NICHOLAS, C. A. C.

pp. [On margin: MAUPIN to HAYS, Deed]
281- THIS INDENTURE made this eleventh day of September in the year of our
282 Lord one thousand seven hundred and ninety four; Between THOMAS MAU-

PIN of the County of Albemarle of the one part and ISAAC HAYS of the same County of the other part; Witnesseth that THOMAS MAUPIN and ANN his Wife in consideration of the sum of seventy five pounds in hand paid to THOMAS MAUPIN and ANN his Wife, the receipt whereof we do hereby acknowledge, have bargained and sold unto ISAAC HAYS one certain tract of land containing two hundred acres lying in the County aforesaid and bounded lying and joining of WILLIAM JARMAN, WILLIAM SHELTON, JOEL PERKINS, BENJAMIN TAYLOR and TARLTON WOODSON, and so including the Plantation whereon JESSE TORREY now lives, which Land THOMAS MAUPIN and ANN his Wife doth convey unto ISAAC HAYS with all houses and appurtnances thereunto belonging; To have and to hold the lands and premises with the appurtenances unto ISAAC HAYS his heirs and THOMAS MAUPIN and ANN his Wife for themselves and their heirs doth by these presents covenant that they shall warrant and defend the land and premises with the appurtenances unto ISAAC HAYS his heirs against the claim of every person, in Witness whereof we have hereunto set our hands and seals the day and year first above written

Signed sealed and delivered in presence of

[no witnesses recorded] THOMAS his mark X MAUPIN
ANN her mark X MAUPIN

Received the day and date of the within written Deed of the within named ISAAC HAYS the sum of seventy five pounds current money of Virginia being in full consideration of the within mentioned land and tenement

THOMAS his mark X MAUPIN
ANN her mark X MAUPIN

At Albemarle September Court 1794

The foregoing Indenture was produced into Court and acknowledged by THOMAS MAUPIN and ANN his Wife, she being first privily examined as the Law directs, and ordered to be recorded Teste JOHN NICHOLAS, C. A. C.

pp. [On margin: MELTON's Trustees to CLARK, Deed]
282- THIS INDENTURE made this fourteenth day of July one thousand seven
283 hundred and ninety four; Between CHARLES L. LEWIS, WILLIAM CLARK, HOWEL LEWIS and EDWARD MOORE a majority of the Trustees of the Town of MELTON by Act of Assembly of one part and WILLIAM CLARK, JUNR. of the County of Albemarle of the other part; Witnesseth that CHARLES L. LEWIS, WILLIAM CLARK, HOWELL LEWIS and EDWARD MOORE by virtue of an Act of Assembly for establishing the Town of MELTON on the lands of BENNETT HENDERSON in the County of Albemarle and in consideration of the sum of fourteen pounds, five shillings current money of Virginia to them in hand paid by WILLIAM CLARK, JUNR. the receipt whereof they do hereby acknowledge hath bargained and sold unto WILLIAM CLARK, JUNR. and to his heirs one certain lott or parcel of land containing half an acre marked in the Plan of the Town number [19] To have and to hold the lott of land with all its appurtenances thereunto belonging unto WILLIAM CLARK, JUNR. his heirs and CHARLES L. LEWIS, WILLIAM CLARK, HOWELL LEWIS and EDWARD MOORE, Trustees aforesaid, do hereby covenant and agree that the lott of ground with appurtenances unto WILLIAM CLARK, JUNR his heirs they shall warrant and by these presents for ever defend, In Witness whereof

CHARLES L. LEWIS, WILLIAM CLARK, HOWELL LEWIS and EDWARD MOORE have hereunto set their hands and affixed their seals the day and year first above written

Signed sealed and delivered in the presence of

JOHN THOMAS,	CHARLES L. LEWIS
WILLIAM D. MERIWETHER	WILLIAM CLARK,
BENNETT HENDERSON	HOWELL LEWIS
JOEL SHIFLETT	EDWARD MOORE

At Albemarle September Court 1794

The foregoing Indenture was produced into Court and proved by the Oaths of JOHN THOMAS, BENNETT HENDERSON and JOEL SHIFLETT, witnesses thereto, and ordered to be recorded Teste JOHN NICHOLAS, C. A. C.

p. [On margin: MELTON's Trustees to OGLESBY, Deed]

283 THIS INDENTURE made this fourteenth day of July in the year of our Lord one thousand seven hundred and ninety four; Between CHARLES L. LEWIS, WILLIAM CLARK, HOWELL LEWIS and EDWARD MOORE a majority of the Trustees for the Town of MELTON by Act of Assembly of the one part and JACOB OGLESBY of the County of Albemarle of the other part; Witnesseth that CHARLES L. LEWIS, WILLIAM CLARK, HOWELL LEWIS and EDWARD MOORE by virtue of an Act of Assembly for establishing the Town of MELTON on the lands of BENNETT HENDERSON in the County of Albemarle and in consideration of the sum of eight pounds current money of Virginia to them in hand paid by JACOB OGLESBY, the receipt whereof they do hereby acknowledge, have bargained and sold unto JACOB OGLESBY and to his heirs one certain lott of land containing half an acre marked in the plan of the Town number [40], To have and to hold the parcel of land unto JACOB OGLESBY and his heirs and the aforesaid Trustees do covenant and agree with JACOB OGLESBY and his heirs the lott of land against the claim of every person will warrant and forever defend by these presents; In Witness whereof CHARLES L. LEWIS, WILLIAM CLARK, HOWELL LEWIS and EDWARD MOORE have hereunto set their hands and affixed their seals the day and year first above written

Signed sealed and delivered in the presence of

JOHN THOMAS,	CHARLES L. LEWIS
JOEL SHIFLETT	WILLIAM CLARK
BENNETT HENDERSON	HOWELL LEWIS
	EDWARD MOORE

At Albemarle September Court 1794

The foregoing Indenture was produced into Court and proved by the Oaths of JOHN THOMAS, JOEL SHIFLETT and BENNETT HENDERSON, witnesses thereto, and ordered to be recorded Teste JOHN NICHOLAS, C. A. C.

p. [On margin: MILLS to MILLS, Release]

284 We the Subscribers as Legatees of DAVID MILLS, deceased, having a right in fee simple to all the land ZACHARIAH MILLS obtained of his Father, the aforesaid DAVID MILLS, deceased, which is hereby acknowledged by ZACHARIAH provided he should die without legal issue do for the consideration of forty shillings

which each of us have received of ZACHARIAH MILLS release all the right title and interest in and to a certain tract of land lying in County of Albemarle on FISHING CREEK which was sold to RICHARD DURRETT by ZACHARIAH MILLS previous to the signing of these presents; Witness our hands this fifteenth November one thousand seven hundred and ninety three

Teste JAMES SCOTT,	WILLIAM BOSWELL	JOSEPH MILLS
CONYERS WHITE	WYATT MILLS	MARY MILLS
DAVID MICHIE	P. WHITE	WILLIAM LANE
CUTHBERT HARDING	LUCY WHITE	MARY LANE
	SALLY MILLS	DAVID MILLS

At Albemarle June Court 1794
The foregoing Indenture was produced into Court and proved by the Oaths of JAMES SCOTT and CUTHBERT HARDING, two of the witnesses thereto, And at September Court, 1794 was further proved by the Oath of CONYERS WHITE, a third witness thereto and ordered to be recorded

Teste JOHN NICHOLAS, C. A. C.

pp. [On margin: MILLS to MILLS Deed]
284- THIS INDENTURE made the fifteenth day of November one thousand seven
285 hundred and ninety three, Between DAVID MILLS and CLOE his Wife of the one part and ZACHARIAH MILLS of the other part; Witnesseth that DAVID MILLS and CLOE his Wife in consideration of the sum of fifty pounds Virginia currency to them in hand paid the receipt whereof they do hereby acknowledge, have and by these presents do bargain and sell unto ZACHARIAH MILLS all their right title interest and claim in a certain tract of land lying in County of Albemarle on the GREAT MOUNTAINS as Legatees of DAVID MILLS, deceased, which tract of land was willed by the last mentioned DAVID MILLS, deceased, to ZACHARIAH, WYATT, DAVID and JOSEPH MILLS his four Sons in equal proportion and the intention of these presents is to vest for the consideration aforesaid all the claim &c. DAVID MILLS may have to the tract of land under the Will of his deceased Father in his Brother, ZACHARIAH MILLS, To have and to hold the land and premises unto ZACHARIAH MILLS his heirs, In Witness whereof the parties have hereunto set their hands and seals the day above written

Signed sealed and delivered in presence of

JAMES SCOTT	DAVID MILLS
DAVID MICHIE	[There are all kinds of scribblings in the place where a signature would be]
CONYERS WHITE	
JOHN PIERCE	

[one more signature lost at the bottom of the page]

At Albemarle June Court 1794
The foregoing Indenture was produced into Court and proved by the Oath of JAMES SCOTT, one of the witnesses thereto, And at September Court 1794, was further proved by theOaths of DAVID MICHIE and CONYERS WHITE, two other of the witnesses thereto, and ordered to be recorded

Test JOHN NICHOLAS, C. A. C.

pp. [On margin: BOLLING to MOORE, Deed. 400 acres delivered with Commis-
285- sion executed for MARY BOLLING]
286 THIS INDENTURE made this thirteenth day of August one thousand seven hundred and ninety four; Between JOHN BOLLING and MARY his Wife of CHESTERFIELD County of the one part and STEPHEN MOORE of the County of Albemarle of the other part; Witnesseth that JOHN BOLLING and MARY his Wife in consideration of the sum of five hundred pounds current money of Virginia to him in hand paid by STEPHEN MOORE, the receipt whereof JOHN BOLLING doth hereby acknowledge, said JOHN BOLLING and his Wife have and by these presents do bargain and sell unto STEPHEN MOORE his heirs all that tract of land containing by estimation five hundred acres be the same more or less situate in the County of Albemarle in the NORTH GARDEN on the North Branch of HARDWARE RIVER and bounded; Begining at a Rock and runing thence on WILLIAM MOORE's and the Estate of CHARLES WARNER LEWIS's line, North thirty five and an half degrees West four hundred and fifteen poles to a Pine, thence on WILLIAM MOORE's and JOHN EVERITT's line South nine degrees West four hundred thirty six poles to pointers, thence a new line North seventy three degrees East three hundred twenty seven poles to the begining, also all the estate right and title of JOHN BOLLING and MARY his Wife of and in the same; To have and to hold te tract of land with the appurtenances unto STEPHEN MOORE his heirs and JOHN BOLLING and his heirs unto STEPHEN MOORE and his heirs the tract of land with its appurtenances will warrant and for ever defend against all persons by these presents; In Witness whereof we have hereunto set our hands and affixed our seals the day and year above written

Signed sealed and delivered in the presence of

CHARLES WINGFIELD, JUNR. — JOHN BOLLING
WILLIAM MOORE, — MARY BOLLING
GEORGE his mark X HIRT
EDWARD BOLLING

At Albemarle September Court 1794
The foregoing Indenture was produced into Court and proved by the Oaths of CHARLES WINGFIELD, JUNR. WILLIAM MOORE and GEORGE HIRT, three of the witnesses thereto, and ordered to be recorded

Teste JOHN NICHOLAS, C. A. C.

pp. [On margin: MAUPIN to MAUPIN, Deed 100 acres]
286- THIS INDENTURE made this seventh day of September in the year of our
287 Lord one thousand seven hundred and ninety four; Between GABRIEL MAUPIN and MARAH his Wife of the County of Albemarle of one part and THOMAS MAUPIN of the County aforesaid of the other part; Witnesseth that GABRIEL MAUPIN and MARAH his Wife in consideration of the sum of seven hundred pounds current money of Virginia to him in hand paid by THOMAS MAUPIN the receipt whereof they do hereby acknowledge, hath and by these presents doth bargain and sell unto THOMAS MAUPIN and to his heirs one certain tract of land containing by estimation one [100] acres more or less situate in Albemarle County and bounded, Begining at WILLIAM MAUPIN's corner and thence along the said line as it runs to a corner of JOHN MAUPIN's red Oak and thence along the said line as it runs to a cor-

ner of BLAND MAUPIN's Hiccory red Oak Walnut and Dogwood and thence as it leads cornering the same and as it leads to the begining, together with all houses and water courses thereunto belonging; To have and to hold the land and premises with the appurtenances and GABRIEL MAUPIN and his heirs for himself and his heirs the land and premises with the appurtenances unto THOMAS MAUPIN his heirs will warrant and forever defend by these presents against any person lawfully claiming any right or title to the same; In Witness whereof GABRIEL MAUPIN and MARAH his Wife hath hereunto set their hands and seals the day and year above written. Signed sealed and delivered in presence of

[no witnesses recorded] GABRIEL MAUPIN
MARAH MAUPIN

Memorandum: That quiet and peaceable possession and seizin of the within land and premises was had and taken by the within named THOMAS MAUPIN of and from the within named GABRIEL MAUPIN on the day and year within written according to form of the within written Deed in presence of

GABRIEL MAUPIN
MARAH MAUPIN

At Albemarle September Court 1794
The foregoing Indenure was produced into Court and acknowledged by GABRIEL MAUPIN and MARY his Wife, she being first privily examined as the Law directs, and ordered to be recorded

Teste JOHN NICHOLAS, C. A. C.

p. [On margin: PATTERSON to McLEAN, Bill of Sale]
287 Have this day sold L. McLEAN of Albemarle a Negro woman named Letty and her two Children named Randolph and Jerry and warrant for ever to him his heirs against all persons whatsoever and for value received from said McLEAN

Teste JEANNE PEEL February 17th 1794
CHARLES his mark BISHAN DAVID PATTERSON

At Albemarle September Court 1794
The foregoing Bill of Sale was produced into Court and proved by the Oath of CHARLES BISHAN, one of the witnesses thereto, and ordered to be recorded

Teste JOHN NICHOLAS, C. A. C.

pp. [On margin: MELTON's Trustees to KEY, two lotts No. 9, 20]
287- THIS INDENTURE made this seventh day of August in the year of our Lord
288 one thousand seven hundred and ninety one; Between EDWARD CARTER, WILSON CARY NICHOLAS, CHARLES LILBURN LEWIS, WILLIAM CLARK, FRANCIS WALKER EDWARD MOORE and HOWELL LEWIS a majority of the Trustees of the Town of MELTON by Act of Assembly of the one part and JAMES KEY of the County of Albemarle of the other part; Witnesseth that EDWARD CARTER, WILSON CARY NICHOLAS, CHARLES LILBURN LEWIS, WILLIAM CLARK, FRANCIS WALKER, EDWARD MOORE and HOWELL LEWIS by virtue of an Act of Assembly for establishing the Town of MELTON on the lands of BENNETT HENDERSON in the County of Albemarle and in consideration of the sum of twenty nine pounds current money of Virginia to them in hand paid by JAMES KEY the receipt whereof they do hereby acknowledge have bargained and

sold unto JAMES KEY certain lotts of land containing one acre marked in the Plan of the Town by the numbers [9 & 20], To have and to hold the lotts of ground with all the appurtenances thereunto belonging to JAMES KEY his heirs and EDWARD CARTER, WILSON C. NICHOLAS, CHARLES L. LEWIS, WILLIAM CLARK, FRANCIS WALKER, EDWARD MOORE and HOWELL LEWIS, Trustees aforesaid for themselves and their heirs against the claim of all persons shall warrant and forever defend, In Witness whereof [the Trustees aforesaid] or a majority of them hath hereunto set their hands and affixed their seals the day and year first above written
Signed sealed and delivered in the presence of

JOHN HENDERSON,	CHARLES L. LEWIS
JACOB OGLESBY	WILLIAM CLARK
WILLIAM HENDERSON	EDWARD MOORE
	HOWELL LEWIS

At Albemarle September Court 1791
The foregoing Indenture was produced into Court and proved by the Oath of JACOB OGLESBY, one of the witnesses thereto, And at June Court 1794, was further proved by the Oath of JOHN HENDERSON, one of the witnesses thereto, And at September Court 1794, was further proved by the Oath of WILLIAM HENDERSON, a third witness thereto, and ordered to be recorded
Teste JOHN NICHOLAS, C. A. C.

pp. [On margin: KEY to FLEMING. Lotts No. 9, & 20, Deed]
288- THIS INDENTURE made this twelfth day of June one thousand seven hun-
289 dred and ninety four; Between JAMES KEY and MARY his Wife of the one part and FLEMING & McCLANAHAN of the other part; Witnesseth that JAMES KEY and MARY his Wife in consideration of the sum of eighteen pounds in hand paid the receipt whereof they do hereby acknowledge, hath and by these presents doth bargain and sell unto FLEMING & McCLANAHAN a Lott in the Town of MELTON number Nine as marked in the Plan containing half acre to them and their heirs, To have and to hold the lott of ground with all appurtenanes thereunto belonging unto FLEMING & McCLANAHAN and to their heirs and JAMES KEY and MARY his Wife doth hereby covenant that the lott of ground with the appurtenances unto FLEMING & McCLANAHAN and their heirs against the claim of all persons will warrant and defend as witness their hands and seals the day and year first above written
Signed sealed and delivered in presence of

JOHN KEY,	JAMES KEY
ELIJAH D. GILLUM	MARY KEY
ACHILLES DOUGLASS	

At Albemarle September Court 1794
The foregoing Indenture was produced into Court and acknowledged by JAMES KEY, party thereto, and ordered to be recorded
Teste JOHN NICHOLAS, C. A. C.

pp. [On margin: PRICE to McCLANAHAN, one lott, Deed]
289- THIS INDENTURE made the twenty third day of April in the year of our Lord
290 one thousand seven hundred and ninety four; Between RICHARD PRICE of

County of Albemarle of one part and JAMES McCLANAHAN of the County aforesaid of the other part; Witnesseth that RICHARD PRICE in consideration of the sum of seventy three pounds, eight shillings and one penny lawfull money of Virginia to him in hand paid the receipt whereof RICHARD PRICE doth hereby acknowledge, hath and by these presents doth bargain and sell unto JAMES McCLANAHAN the whole of the house and lott of ground in MELTON Kitchen Garden and Stable now in the possession of FLEMING & McCLANAHAN, To have and to hold the lott Kitchen Garden and Stable and all and singular the bargained premises unto JAMES McCLANAHAN and to his heirs; In Witness whereof I have hereunto set my hand and affixed my seal this twenty third day of April A D one thousand seven hundred and ninety four

Sealed and delivered in the presence of
HUGH McALESTER, RICHARD PRICE
ROBERT FLEMING

At Albemarle September Court 1794
The foregoing Indenture was produced into Court and acknowledged by RICHARD PRICE, party thereto, and ordered to be recorded
Teste JOHN NICHOLAS, C. A. C.

p. [On margin: COLEMAN to FITZGERALD 169 1/2 acres. Deed. Delivered
290 WILLIAM WOOD per order]

THIS INDENTURE made this fifth day of September in the year of our Lord one thousand seven hundred and ninety four; Between JAMES COLEMAN of the County of Albemarle of the one part and BARTLETT FITZGERALD [alias] BARTLETT HAWKINS of the said County of the other part; Witnesseth that JAMES COLEMAN in consideration of the sum of ten shillings in hand paid to JAMES COLEMAN, the receipt whereof he doth hereby acknowledge, hath bargained and sold unto BARTLETT FITZGERALD [alias] BARTLETT HAWKINS a certain tract of land containing one hundred and sixty nine and one half acres lying in County of Albemarle and on the Branches of SPRING CREEK and bounded; lying joining of DAVID MILLS, deceased, WILLIAM MOORE, WILLIAM JARMAN and JOHN BRUMFIELD's lines and being part of a tract of land containing three hundred and fifteen and an half acres which Patent bears date the 20th of March one thousand seven hundred and ninety two which land JAMES COLEMAN doth convey unto BARTLETT FITZGERALD [alias] BARTLETT HAWKINS with all houses and appurtenances thereunto belonging; To have and to hold the land and premises with the appurtenances thereunto beloning unto BARTLETT FITZGERALD [alias] BARTLETT HAWKINS his heirs and JAMES COLEMAN and his heirs against the claim of every person will warrant and forever defend by these presents; In Witness whereof I have hereunto set my hand and affixed my seal the day and year first above written

Signed sealed and delivered in presence of
JUDITH COLEMAN, JAMES his mark X COLEMAN
WILLIAM JOHNSON,
SUSAN JOHNSON,
WILLIAM PERKINS

Received the day and date of the within mentioned Deed the sum of ten shillings from BARTLETT FITZGERALD [alias] BARTLETT HAWKINS in full consideration of the within mentioned land and tenements

Teste WILLIAM JOHNSON, JAMES his mark X COLEMAN
SUSANNA JOHNSON
JUDITH COLEMAN,
WILLIAM PERKINS

At Albemarle September Court 1794
The foregoing Indenture was produced into Court and proved by the Oath of JUDITH COLEMAN, WILLIAM JOHNSON and WILLIAM PERKINS, three of the witnesses thereto and ordered to be recorded
Teste JOHN NICHOLAS, C. A. C.

p. [On margin: BOLES to SQUIRE, Deed. 200 acres]
291 THIS INDENTURE made this ninth day of June one thousand seven hundred and ninety four; Between NATHAN BOWLES and MILDRED his Wife of the one part and ANDREW SQUAIRS of the other part; Witnesseth that NATHAN BOWLES and MILDRED his Wife in consideration of sum of one hundred pounds current money of Virginia to them in hand paid by ANDREW SQUAIRS the receipt whereof is hereby acknowledgeed, hath bargained and sold unto ANDREW SQUAIRS and to his heirs one certain tract of land lying in County of Albemarle on TOTIER CREEK containing by estimation two hundred acres and bounded; Begining at a Pine corner to ARTHUR WHITE, thence South fifty seven degrees West seventeen poles to pointers corner to MARTIN DAWSON, thence South thirty seven degrees East two hundred and eighty nine poles to a Pine, thence South fourteen and an half degrees West seventy five poles to a Hickory, thence North sixty degrees East one hundred and ten poles to pointers, thence East fifty poles to a white Oak by a Pine, thence with the North Fork of TOTIER CREEK eighty poles to a Maple in the Fork of a Branch, thence North fifty eight degrees West three hundred and eighty five poles to the begining; To have and to hold the tract of land with all the appurtenances thereunto belonging unto ANDREW SQUAIRS and to his heirs and NATHAN BOWLES for himself and his heirs the land and premises unto ANDREW SQUAIRS his heirs against the claim of every person will warrant and forever defend by these presents; In Witness whereof I have hereunto set my hand and affixed my seal the day and year first above written

Signed sealed and delivered in presence of
WILLIAM his mark X GOOLSBY NATHAN BOWLES
JOHN CLARKSON
WILLIAM CLARKSON

At Albemarle September Vourt 1794
The foregoing Indenture was produced into Court and acknowledged by NATHAN BOWLES, party thereto, and ordered to be recorded
Teste JOHN NICHOLAS, C. A. C.

pp. [On margin: NICHOLAS to TAZEWELL, Deed. 1300 acres]
291- THIS INDENTURE made this twenty third day of September in the year of
293 our Lord one thousand seven hundred and ninety three; Between WILSON CARY NICHOLAS of the County of Albemarle of the one part and HENRY

TAZEWELL of County of JAMES CITY of the other part; Whereas WILSON CARY NICHOLAS stands indebted unto HENRY TAZEWELL by Bond in the just and full sum of three thousand pounds with Interest from the date hereof for securing the payment whereof this Indenture Witnesseth that WILSON CARY NICHOLAS in consideration of the sum of five shillings by HENRY TAZEWELL to him in hand paid the receipt whereof WILSON CARY NICHOLAS doth acknowledge, and for the consideration of the Debt aforesaid, WILSON CARY NICHOLAS hath and by these presents doth bargain and sell unto HENRY TAZEWELL his heirs all that tract of land situate in County of Albemarle containing one thousand three hundred acres on the East side of BALLENGER's CREEK bounded on the South and West by JAMES RIVER and BALLENGER's CREEK, on the North and East by a line to the Run from JAMES RIVER at a Gut which is at the lower end of the said NICHOLAS's Meadow out into the Forest and so to BALLENGER's CREEK to include one hundred and fifty acres of River Low Ground and eleven hundred and fifty acres of high land adjoining thereto, part of which land WILSON CARY NICHOLAS had from his Father and the other part thereof from his Brother, JOHN NICHOLAS, it being the land whereon WILSON CARY NICHOLAS now lives together with all houses, mills, water courses and appurtenances to the same belonging; To have and to hold all and singular the premises with the appurtenances unto HENRY TAZEWELL his heirs and by these presents for ever warrant and defend, provided always and these presents are upon this condition that if WILSON CARY NICHOLAS his heirs shall well and truly pay or cause to be paid unto HENRY TAZEWELL his heirs the just and full sum of three thousand pounds with the Interest accruing thereon as the same shall be due and payable then these presents and everything therein contained shall cease and become void otherwise shall remain in full force and virtue; In Witness whereof the parties to these presents have hereunto set their hands and affixed their seals this twenty third day of September in the year of our Lord one thousand seven hundred and ninety three

Sealed and delivered in the presence of us
WILLIAM TOMPKINS — WILSON CARY NICHOLAS
LITTR: W. TAZEWELL,
MATHEW JORDAN

Memo: Any lotts which the said NICHOLAS may have sold but not conveyed in the Town of WARREN are excepted out of this conveyance

Witness WILLIAM TOMPKINS — HENRY TAZEWELL
LITTR: W. TAZEWELL
MATHEW JORDAN

April 12th 1794. Acknowledged before — DAVID BULLOCK
ROBERT JOUETT
FRANCIS TALIAFERRO

At Albemarle September Court 1794

The foregoing Indenture was produced into Court and acknowledged by WILSON CARY NICHOLAS, party thereto, and ordered to be recorded

Teste JOHN NICHOLAS, C. A. C.

pp. [On margin: KEISTER to KEISTER, Deed. 100 acres]
293- THIS INDENTURE made and done this third day of October one thousand
294 seven hundred and ninety four; Between PHILIP KEISTER of County of AUGUSTA of the one part and JOHN KEISTER of County of ORANGE of the other part; Witnesseth that PHILIP KEISTER for sundry good causes and considerations but more especially in consideration of the full and just sum of one hundred pounds current money of Virginia to him in hand paid the receipt whereof I do hereby acknowledge, hath and by these presents doth bargain and sell unto JOHN KEISTER and his heirs all that tract of land lying in County of Albemarle and bounded, Begining at a small Hiccory saplin corner to JOHN GRAVES thence North fifty five degrees West one hundred and forty five poles to two Maples and a Pine in a Branch in SANFORD's Old Line, thence South forty five degrees West one hundred and eighty poles to three red Oaks and two Hiccory pointers thence South nineteen degrees West seventy eight poles to a Pine on the spur of PINEY MOUNTAIN, thence East one hundred and thirty poles to a white Oak Stump corner to JOHN CROSTHWAIT, thence North seven degrees East one hundred poles to two Pines corner to WILLIAM HALL, thence South fifty eight degrees East eighty eight poles to a Stake corner to JOHN GRAVES, from thence to the first station, containing by estimation one hundred acres, together with all houses orchards gardens and water courses with their appurtenances and the rents issues and profits thereof; To have and to hold the land and premises with their appurtenances unto JOHN KEISTER his heirs and to the use profits benefit and advantage of JOHN KEISTER his heirs and for no other use, and I do forever warrant and defend the tract of land against all claims that shall hereafter appear, In Witness whereof I have hereunto set my hand and seal the day and year first above written

Signed sealed and delivered in presence of
JOHN D. GRYMES, PHILIP KEISTER
JAMES BROWN,
PETER [? WILSIN]

Received of JOHN KEISTER one hundred pounds current money of Virginia in full according to the form and effect of the within Deed this day and year within written
Teste JOHN D. GRYMES PHILIP KEISTER

At Albemarle October Court 1794
The foregoing Indenture was produced into Court and acknowledged by PHILIP KEISTER, party thereto, and ordered to be recorded
Teste JOHN NICHOLAS, C. A. C.

pp. [On margin: JOHNSON to HISER, Deed, 130 acres]
294- THIS INDENTURE made the tenth day of March in the year of our Lord one
295 thousand seven hundred and ninety four; Between WILLIAM JOHNSON and LETTY his Wife of County of Albemarle of one part and SAMUEL HISER of County of AUGUSTA of the other part; Witnesseth that WILLIAM JOHNSON and LETTY his Wife for divers good causes and considerations but more especially for the sum of sixty pounds current money of Virginia to him in hand paid by SAMUEL HISER the receipt whereof he doth hereby acknowledge hath and by these presents doth bargain and sell unto SAMUEL HISER his heirs a certain tract of land lying in County of Albemarle on some of the head waters of ROCKFISH containing one hun-

dred and thirty acres be the same more or less and bounded, Begining at a white Oak on ANDREW KEITH's line runing thence on his line North eighty seven degrees East one hundred and twenty poles to a Branch, same course twenty eight poles to a Locust, North twenty one degrees West eight poles to a Branch, same course seventy poles to a red Oak, North twenty nine degrees East twelve poles to a red Oak, North nineteen degrees West twenty four poles to a Chesnut Oak saplin, South seventy nine degrees West sixty poles to a Branch, same course ninety two poles to a Hiccory on ANDREW KEITH's line, South twenty nine degrees East one hundred and forty poles to the begining; To have and to hold the tract of land with its appurtenances unto SAMUEL HISER his heirs and WILLIAM JOHNSON for himself and his heirs the tract of land with its appurtenances unto SAMUEL HISER his heirs against all persons will warrant and by these presents for ever defend; In Witness whereof WILLIAM JOHNSON and LETTY his Wife hath hereunto set their hands and seals the day and year above written
Signed sealed and delivered in presence of

JAMES ANDERSON, WILLIAM JOHNSON
JOHN DILLER, LETTICE JOHNSON
JOHN HEIZER

At Albemarle October Court 1794
The foregoing Indenture was produced into Court and acknowledged by WILLIAM JOHNSON and LETTICE his Wife, she being first privily examined as the Law directs, and ordered to be recorded

Teste JOHN NICHOLAS C. A. C.

p. [On margin: MAUPIN to MAUPIN Deed, 50 acres]
295 THIS INDENTURE made this ninth day of October in the year of our Lord one thousand seven hundred and ninety four; Between WILLIAM MAUPIN of the one part and BLAND MAUPIN of the other part each of the County of Albemarle, Witnesseth that WILLIAM MAUPIN in consideration of the sum of fifty pounds current money to him in hand paid by BLAND MAUPIN the receipt whereof he doth hereby acknowledge hath and by these presents doth bargain and sell unto BLAND MAUPIN and to his heirs one certain tract of land containing fifty acres being in County of Albemarle and bounded on WILLIAM MAUPIN's lands on the South and others begining at a corner adjoining WILLIAM MAUPIN's lands at a large Poplar and Spanish Oak and continuing thence North forty degrees East one hundred and ten poles to a corner Stake, thence South sixty degrees East eighty poles to a corner Pine Stump, thence South forty degrees West forty two poles to a Dogwood, thence seventy dgrees West ninety one poles to the begining; To have and to hold the tract of land to him and his heirs and WILLIAM MAUPIN doth for himself and his heirs warrant and defend the premises to BLAND MAUPIN his heirs against the claim of every person, In Witness whereof WILLIAM MAUPIN hath hereunto set his hand and affixed his seal the day and year first above written
Signed sealed and delivered in presence of

[no witnesses recorded] WILLIAM MAUPIN

At Albemarle October Court 1794
The foregoing Indenture was produced into Court and acknowledgedby WILLIAM MAUPIN, party thereto and ordered to be recorded Teste JOHN NICHOLAS CAC

pp. [On margin: MAUPIN to MAUPIN, Deed. 175 acres]
295- THIS INDENTURE made this seventh day of October one thousand seven
296 hundred and ninety four; Between THOMAS MAUPIN and ANNA his Wife of the County of Albemarle of the one part and GABRIEL MAUPIN of the same County of the other part; Witnesseth that THOMAS MAUPIN and ANNA his Wife in consideration of he sum of seven hundred pounds current money of Virginia to him in hand paid by GABRIEL MAUPIN, the receipt whereof THOMAS MAUPIN and ANNA his Wife doth hereby acknowledge hath and by these presents doth bargain and sell unto GABRIEL MAUPIN his heirs one certain tract of land containing by supposition one hundred and seventy five acres more or less lying in Albemarle County and situated under and on the GREAT MOUNTAINS on the Branches of ROCKY CREEK and bounded; Begining upon the top of the Mountain at WILLIAM WOOD's line cornering on a Pine and thence along the said line and runing to a corner of WILLIAM DUNN's, and thence along the said line as it runs to WILLIAM BRUCE's lower line and thence along the said line as it runs to WILLIAM WOOD cornering there and thence along the said line as it runs to the top of the Mountain at the begining, together with all houses orchards and water courses thereunto belonging, To have and to hold the land and premises with all appurtenances to the same belonging unto THOMAS MAUPIN his heirs and THOMAS MAUPIN for himself and heirs the land and premises with appurtenances to GABRIEL MAUPIN his heirs will warrant and for ever defend by these presents against any person claiming any right or title to the same; In Witness whereof THOMAS MAUPIN and ANNA his Wife hath hereunto set their hands and seals the day and date above written

Signed sealed and delivered in presence of
[no witnesses recorded] THOMAS his mark X MAUPIN

At Albemarle October Court 1794
The foregoing Indenture was produced into Court and acknowledged by THOMAS MAUPIN, party thereto, and ordered to be recorded
Teste JOHN NICHOLAS, C. A. C.

pp. [On margin: THACKER to BARKSDALE, Deed. 138 acres. Delivered to
297- SAMUEL BARKSDALE]
298 THIS INDENTURE made this [blank] day of July in the year of our Lord one thousand seven hundred and ninety four; Between AMBROSE THACKER and MARY THACKER his Wife of the County of Albemarle of one part and SAMUEL BARKSDALE of the same County of the other part; Witnesseth that AMBROSE THACKER and MARY THACKER his Wife in consideration of the sum of five pounds current money of Virginia to him in hand paid by SAMUEL BARKSDALE the receipt whereof AMBROSE THACKER and MARY THACKER his Wife doth hereby acknowledge, hath and by these presents doth bargain and sell unto SAMUEL BARKSDALE his heirs a tract of land containing one hundred and thirty eight acres lying on the South side of the RAGGED MOUNTAINS in the County of Albemarle bounded by JOHN WHARTON and HENRY WILLIAMS and the said SAMUEL BARKSDALE and the reversions and remainders thereof, To have and to hold the land and premises with appurtenances unto SAMUEL BARKSDALE his heirs and AMBROSE THACKER and MARY THACKER his Wife and their heirs against all other persons

will warrant and defend by these presents; In Witness whereof we to these presents our hands and seals have set and affixed the day and year above written
Signed sealed and delivered in presence of

[no witnesses recorded] AMBROSE his mark X THACKER
MARY her mark X THACKER

Memo: That on the day and year within written full possession and seizin was had and taken of the land and premises within granted by the within named AMBROSE THACKER and MARY THACKER and by them delivered over unto the within named SAMUEL BARKSDALE to hold to him his heirs &c. according to the contracts and true meaning of the within written Indenture

AMBROSE his mark X THACKER
MARY her mark X THACKER

At Albemarle October Court 1794
The foregoing Indenture was produced into Court and acknowledged by AMBROSE THACKER, one of the parties thereto, and ordered to be recorded
Teste JOHN NICHOLAS, C. A. C.

p. 298 [On margin: WILKINSON &c. to DURRETT, Deed. 51 acres. Delivered to McKENZIE]

THIS INDENTURE made the first day of March in the year of our Lord one thousand seven hundred and ninety four, Between JOHN WILKINSON and ANDREW HART both of the County of Albemarle of one part and MARSHALL DURRETT of the County aforesaid of the other part; Witnesseth that JOHN WILKINSON and ANDREW HART in consideration of the sum of eleven pounds, nine shillings and six pence in hand paid hath bargained and sold unto MARSHALL DURRETT his heirs a certain tract of land in the County of Albemarle and on the waters of MECHUM's RIVER and bounded; Begining at a red Oak in DAVID BURGESS's line and runing with his line above one hundred poles to pointers corner to DAVID BURGESS in MARSHALL DURRETT's line, then on DURRETT's line North forty five degrees East twenty eight poles to a black Oak corner to said DURRETT, thence North eighty five degrees East one hundred and twelve poles to a Spanish Oak in DANIEL WHITE's line, then two hundred and ten poles to the begining; containing fifty one acres be the same more or less, To have and to hold the land and premises with appurtenances unto MARSHALL DURRETT his heirs and JOHN WILKINSON and ANDREW HART doth covenant and oblige themselves their heirs to warrant and defend the tract of land unto MARSHALL DURRETT his heirs, In Witness whereof JOHN WILKINSON and ANDREW HART have assigned their hands and affixed their seals the day and year above written
Signed sealed and delivered in the presence of

[no witnesses recorded] JOHN WILKINSON
A. HART

At Albemarle October Court 1794
The foregoing Indenture was produced into Court and acknowledged by JOHN WILKINSON and ANDREW HART, parties thereto, and ordered to be recorded
Teste JOHN WILKINSON, C. A. C.

pp. [On margin: WILKINSON. to McKENZIE Deed, 100 acres]
298- THIS INDENTURE made the fifteenth day of May in the year of our Lord one
299 thousand seven hundred and ninety four; Between JOHN WILKINSON of the County of Albemarle of one part and DONALD McKENZIE of the County of AMHERST of the other part; Witnesseth that JOHN WILKINSON in consideration of the sum of thirty four pounds current money of Virginia to him in hand paid, the receipt whereof is hereby acknowledged, hath bargained and sold unto DONALD McKENZIE and to his heirs one certain tract of land lying in County of Albemarle on the waters of CARR CREEK containing one hundred acres be the same more or less and bounded; Begining at a Hiccory corner to GEORGE BLAINE and runing thence South sixty one degrees West one hundred and twenty two poles to a white Oak Stump in GEORGE BLAINE'S line, thence North three degrees East on said BLAINE's line and after on SAMUEL MINRAL's line one hundred and seventy poles to pointers in a survey of the said WILKINSON, thence a straight line to the begining; together with all and singular the appurtenances thereunto belonging; To have and to hold the tract of land with appurtenances unto DONALD McKENZIE and his heirs, and JOHN WILKINSON doth hereby covenant and agree to and with DONALD McKENZIE that the tract of land and premises with all appurtenances a clear and fee simple title therein to DONALD McKENZIE his heirs shall warrant and forever defend by these presents; In Witness whereof I have hereunto set my hand and seal the day and year first above written

Signed sealed and delivered in presence of
CHARLES McALESTER, JOHN WILKINSON
JOHN McCLURE,
WILLIAM HART,
WILLIAM HARLOW

Memorandum: that on the day and year within written quiet and peaceable possession and seizen was had by JOHN WILKINSON of the within land and by him delivered to the within named DONALD McKENZIE according to the true intent and meaning of the within Indenture, In presence of
JOHN McCLURE, JOHN WILKINSON
CHARLES McALESTER
WILLIAM HART
WILLIAM HARLOW

At Albemarle October Court 1794
The foregoing Indenture was produced into Court and acknwledged by JOHN WILKINSON, party thereto, and ordered to be recorded
Teste JOHN NICHOLAS, C. A. C.

pp. [On margin: HARVIE to BATES, Deed. 600 acres]
299- THIS INDENTURE made this twenty sixth day of March one thousand seven
300 hundred and ninety four; Between JOHN HARVIE and MARY his Wife of County of RICHMOND of the one part and MOSES BATES of the County of CHESTERFIELD of the other part; Witnesseth that JOHN HARVIE and MARY his Wife in consideration of sum of eighty pounds to him in hand paid the receipt whereof is hereby acknowledged, hath and by these presents doth bargain and sell unto MOSES BATES his heirs a certain tract of land lying in County of Albemarle on IVY

CREEK containing by a Survey made by JOHN SLAUGHTER six hundred acres be the same more or less and is bounded, Begining at a dead Pine on a Hill side supposed to be a corner of GEORGE WAYTE's thence South twenty eight East one hundred and twenty poles to a Post Oak, thence South sixteen West one hundred and twenty six poles to a red Oak and a white Oak on the bank of IVY CREEK where GEORGE WAYTE's line crosses the Creek, then down the Creek with the several meanders thereof East thirty poles, North eighty four East fifty eight poles, North thirty West fourteen poles, North sixty five West twenty six poles, North fifteen East eighteen poles, North seventy East twenty poles, North twenty seven North fifty five East fourteen poles North thirty two poles, South fifty one East forty six poles, North five East eighteen poles, South sixty one East forty four poles to a large white Oak on the bank of the Creek upon the North side and then leaving the Creek with BURCH's line South six West sixty six poles to a white Oak on the side of BURCH's Fence then along the same South sixty four East seventy six poles to a bending Poplar on the side of a large Branch, then crossing the Branch North twenty three East fifty poles to a red Oak and Spanish Oak pointers on a Hill side come to PHILLIPS's and GRADY's thence with GRADY's line North thirty three West two hundred fifteen poles to a white Oak corner on the side of the BARRACK ROAD in GRADY's line, then along the Road North sixty five West thirty two poles, thence North thirty West forty poles, thence South three West fifty two poles, North fifteen West five poles to two Maples on the bank of IVY CREEK, North thirty West fifty one poles, thence North thirty two West thirty two poles, then North forty one West forty four poles to a small Post Oak in the Fork of the Road, then South fifty four West three hundred forty two poles to the begining; To have and to hold the tract of land and premises with appurtenances to MOSES BATES and his heirs and JOHN HARVIE for himself and his heirs doth covenant with MOSES BATES his heirs to warrant and defend the tract of land against the claim of every person; In Witness whereof JOHN HARVIE hath hereunto affixed his hand and seal the day and year above written

In presence of

MARTHA SNEED, JOHN HARVIE
POLLY GARTH,
GEORGE WINSTON

At Albemarle July Court 1794

The foregoing Indenture was produced into Court and proved by the Oaths of MARTHA SNEED and POLLY GARTH, two of the witnesses thereto, And at October Court was acknowledged by JOHN HARVIE, party thereto, and ordered to be recorded Teste JOHN NICHOLAS, C. A. C.

pp. [On margin: SMITH to SMITH, Deed. 223 acres. Delivered to J. SMITH]
300- THIS INDENTURE made this fourth day of October in the year of our Lord
301 one thousand seven hundred and ninety four; Between JOHN SMTH, Captain,
of County of Albemarle of the one part and JOEL SMITH of said County of the other part; Witnesseth that JOHN SMITH, Capt., in consideration of the sum of seventy five pounds current money of Virginia to him in hand paid by JOEL SMITH, the receipt whereof JOHN SMITH, Capt., doth hereby acknowledge, hath and by these presents doth bargain and sell unto JOEL SMITH and his heirs one certain tract of land containing two hundred and twenty three acres of land lying in the Coun-

ty of Albemarle on the Branches of ROCKFISH and MICHUM's RIVERs and bounded, Begining at a Gum in CHARLES SMITH's line thence South eight degrees East fifty poles to a Spanish Oak, South twenty five degrees West fifty poles to a Spanish Oak, South five degrees East fifty eight poles to a Chesnut tree and pointers, South thirteen degrees East eighty poles to a Hiccory, South sixty two degrees East thirty eight poles to a dead Chesnut tree and pointers, South thirteen degrees East eighty poles to a Hiccory, South sixty two degrees East thirty eight poles to a dead Chesnut tree and pointers on the Old Patent Line, South sixty six degrees East fifty six poles to pointers, South thirteen degrees East fifty one poles to a Sassafras, North sixty three degrees East twenty two poles to a Hiccory, North sixteen degrees East ninety eight poles to a Chesnut tree, thence along ISAAC WOOD's line on top of a Ridge along to a large white Oak and from thence a straight line to the begining; and now in the possession of JOEL SMITH, and all right title claim and demand of JOHN SMITH, Capt. To have and to hold the land and premises with the appurtenances unto JOEL SMITH and his heirs and JOHN SMITH Capt. will warrant and forever defend by these presents. In witness whereof JOHN SMITH, Capt. hath hereunto set his hand and seal the day and year above written

Signed sealed and delivered in presence of

NICHOLAS BURGER, JOHN SMITH, SENR.

JOHN PATRICK,

THOMAS SMITH,

KELLIS CHEWNING, SAMUEL PATTERSON

WILLIAM SMITH, DANIEL WHITE

Received of JOEL SMITH the sum of seventy five pounds being the consideration of the within mentioned this 4th day of October 1794

JOHN SMITH, SENR.

At Albemarle October Court 1794

The foregoing Indenture was produced into Court and proved by the Oaths of NICHOLAS BURGER, WILLIAM SMITH and DANIEL WHITE, three of the witnesses thereto, and ordered to be recorded

Test JOHN NICHOLAS, C. A. C.

p. [On margin: OWENS to LEWIS, Bill of Sale]

302 KNOW ALL MEN by these presents that I WILLIAM OWENS of the County of Albemarle have bargained and sold JAMES LEWIS of the said County two horses, the one a bay Mare about three years old the ensuing Spring, about four feet six or seven inches high branded on the near shoulder and buttock W the other a bay Mare Colt two years old this Spring branded on the near shoulder W., about six feet seven inches high, two Cows, the one a red Cow mixed with white and branded about three years old marked with a crop slit and underkeel in the right ear and slit and underkeel in the left, the other a reddish coloured Cow not marked about four years old with short horns, ten hoggs marked with the same marks as the first mentioned Cow, two feather beds and furniture, one Rifle Gun and the one half which I own in the Stud, Federalist, which property I warrant and defend to JAMES LEWIS his heirs against the claim of every person, In Witness whereof I have hereunto set my hand and seal this 24th day of February 1794. The Condition of the above is such that if the above bound WILLIAM OWENS his heirs &c. shall pay unto JAMES

LEWIS his heirs on or before the fifteenth day of September next fifty pounds Virginia currency and fifty pounds Virginia currency on or before the fifteenth day of September 1795 and deliver the stud horse up to JAMES LEWIS when called for, then the above Obligation to be void or else to remain in full force and virtue
Signed sealed and delivered in presence of
JOHN BUSTER, WILLIAM OWENS
RICHARD BURCH
At Albemarle October Court 1794
The foregoing Bill of Sale was produced into Court and proved by the Oaths of JOHN BUSTER and RICHARD BURCH, the witnesses thereto, and ordered to be recorded
Teste JOHN NICHOLAS, C. A. C.

p. [On margin; STATHAM to JOHNSON, Bill of Sale]
302 This day bargained sold and delivered unto RICHARD JOHNSON one bay Horse I got of JOHN EVERITT and one Negro girl by the name of Jean which I got by my Wife for the consideration of eighteen pounds to me in hand paid, which property I forever defend from me my heirs, the above Obligation is such that if the said DABNEY pays or causes to be paid unto RICHARD JOHNSON the just sum of eighteen pounds current money of Virginia with Interest on or beforethe last day of May next the above obligation to be void or lese to remain in full force and virtue; Given under my hand and seal this 15th day of March 1794
Teste JAMES CARDIN, WILLIAM D. STATHAM
BENJAMIN JOHNSON
WILLIAM HUMPHREY
At Albemarle October Court 1794
The foregoing Bill of Sale was produced into Court and proved by the Oaths of JAMES CARDIN and BENJAMIN JOHNSON, two of the witnesses thereto, and ordered to be recorded Teste JOHN NICHOLAS, C. A. C.

p. [On margin: GARLAND to ELSOM, Deed. 9 acres. Examined and delivered
303 per Order]
THIS INDENTURE made this first day of October in the year of our Lord one thouand seven hundred and ninety four; Between JAMES GARLAND late Sheriff of Albemarle County of one part and WILLIAM ELSOM of the County aforesaid of the other part; Witnesseth that agreeable to an Act of Assembly passed in the year one thousand seven hundred and ninety two directing that the then acting Sheriff should by publick auction expose to sale certain publick lands for the payment of the Tax due thereon and further directing that the said Sheriff should for and on behalf of the Commonwealth make a Deed thereby conveying to the purchaser a fee simple right to the said lands so sold under the direction of that Law. Now the said JAMES GARLAND, as Sheriff, and by virtue of the aforesaid Act in consideration of the sum of two pounds, four shillings the same for which the said land sold and by these presents bargain and sell unto WILLIAM ELSOM a certain tract of land being part of THOMAS COLDER's Old Tract lying in County of Albemarke and is bounded, Begining at pointers on BENJAMIN JORDAN's line runing South seventy four degrees East thirty eight poles to pointers, South twenty degrees West thirty eight ples to a red Oak, North ninety four degrees West thirty eight poles to red Oak, North twenty

degrees East thirty eight poles to the first station, which parcel of land JAMES GARLAND as Sheriff and by virture of the recited Law do bargain sell and convey unto WILLIAM ELSOM with all appurtenances thereunto belonging unto him and his heirs and JAMES GARLAND for himself and his heirs doth warrant and defend the tract of land from any person claiming the same, Given under my hand and seal as Sheriff this first day of October and year above written

JAMES GARLAND

At Albemarle October Court 1794
The foregoing Indenture was produced into Court and acknowledged by JAMES GARLAND, party thereto, and ordered to be recorded

Teste JOHN NICHOLAS, C. A. C.

pp. [On margin: GARLAND, Sheriff to BUSTER, Deed. 50 acres]
303- THIS INDENTURE made this ninth day of October in the year of our Lord one
304 thousand seven hundred and ninety four; Between JAMES GARLAND, late Sheriff of Albemarle County, of one part and JOHN BUSTER of the County aforesaid of the other part; Witnesseth that agreeable to an Act of Assembly passed in the year one thousand seven hundred and ninety two, directing that the then acting Sheriff should by publick auction expose to sale certain publick lands for the payment of Taxes thereon and further directing that the Sheriff should for and on behalf of the Commonwealth make a Deed hereby conveying to the purchasers a fee simple right to the lands so sold under the direction of the said Law, and now JAMES GARLAND as Sheriff and by virtue of the recited Act in consideration of the sum of three pounds one and six pence, the sum for which the land sold hath by these presents bargained and sold unto JOHN BUSTER a certain parcel of land being a part of WILLIAM MARTIN's Tract lying in County of Albemarle containing fifty acres and it bounded, Begining at pointers on OBEDIAH BRITT's line, thence runing North eighty six and one half degrees East ninety poles to pointers, South fourteen degrees West ninety poles to a white Oak, South eighty six degrees and a half West ninety poles to pointers, North fourteen and a half degrees East ninety poles to the begining; which parcel of land JAMES GARLAND as Sheriff and by virtue of the recited Law do bargain sell and convey unto JOHN BUSTER with all and singular the appurtenances thereunto belonging to him and his heirs, and JAMES GARLAND for himself and his heirs do warrant and defend the tract of land from any person claiming the same, Given under my hand and seal as Sheriff the ninth day of October and the year above written

JAMES GARLAND

At Albemarle October Court 1794
The foregoing Indenture was produced into Court and acknowledged by JAMES GARLAND, party thereto, and ordered to be recorded

Teste JOHN NICHOLAS C. A. C.

pp. [On margin: TURNER to VIA, Ded. 113 acres]
304- THIS INDENTURE made this twenty fifth day of September one thousand
305 seven hundred and ninety four; Between ROBERT TURNER of the County of Albemarle of one part and WAID VIA of the same County of the other part; Witnesseth that in consideration of the sum of forty five pounds current money of

Virginia to him in hand paid the receipt whereof he doth hereby acknowledge, hath bargained and sold unto WAID VIA and his heirs one certain tract of land lying in County of Albemarle containing one hundred and thirteen acres of land on the Branches of MECHUM's RIVER bounded by DANIEL MAUPIN, JOHN BENT and others being part of a tract that was formerly SOLOMON BALEW's To have and to hold the tract of land and premises with all and singular the appurtenances unto WAID VIA his heirs and ROBERT TURNER for himself his heirs doth covenant with WAID VIA that the tract of land and premises with all appurtenances shall and will warrant and for ever defend by these presents, In Witness whereof he hath hereunto set his hand and affixed his seal the day and year first mentioned
Signed sealed and delivered in presence of

MICAJAH VIA — ROBERT TURNER
ROWLAND HORSLEY
WILLIAM BALLARD

At Albemarle October Court 1794
The foregoing Indenture was produced into Court and proved by the Oaths of MICAJAH VIA, ROWLAND HORSLEY and WILLIAM BALLARD, witnesses thereto, and ordered to be recorded Test JOHN NICHOLAS, C. A. C.

p. [On margin: BRUCE to GILLUM, Deed. 1 lott No. 44.]
305 THIS INDENTURE made this twenty sixth day of July in the year of our Lord one thousand seven hundred and ninety four; Between GEORGE BRUCE and TEMPERANCE BRUCE both of the County of Albemarle of one part and ELISHA D. GILLUM of said County of the other part; Witnesseth that GEORGE BRUCE in consideration of the sum of fifteen pounds current money to him in hand paid by ELISHA D. GILLUM the receipt whereof he doth hereby acknowledge, hath bargained and sold unto ELISHA D. GILLUM and his heirs one certain lott or land in the Town of MELTON containing one half acre known by the number [44] forty four as marked in the Plat of the Town, To have and to hold the lott of land with all and singular the appurtenances unto ELISHA D. GILLUM and to his heirs and GEORGE BRUCE and TEMPERANCE BRUCE doth hereby covenant and agree that the lott of ground with all its appurtenances unto ELISHA D. GILLUM his heirs that GEORGE BRUCE and TEMPERANCE BRUCE for themselves and their heirs against the claim of any person will warrant and forever defend by these presents, In Witness whereof GEORGE BRUCE and TEMPERANCE BRUCE hath hereunto set their hands and affixed their seals the day and year first above written
Signed sealed and delivered in presence of

WILLIAM CLARK, — GEORGE BRUCE
JOEL SHIFLETT, — TEMPERANCE BRUCE
WILLIAM CLARK, JUNR.

At Albemarle October Court 1794
The foregoing Indenture was produced into Court and acknowledged by GEORGE BRUCE, party thereto, and ordered to be recorded
Teste JOHN NICHOLAS, C. A. C.

pp. [On margin: BUCKNER to JOHNSON, Power of Attorney]
305- KNOW YE that placeing especial trust and confidence in my Friend, ROBERT

306 JOHNSON of KENTUCKY I do hereby constitute and appoint the said JOHNSON my lawful Attorney in fact to sell and receive the money and convey for me thirty and a half acres of land being my half of a tract of land containing sixty one acres which land was entered surveyed and Patented in the names of ROBERT JOHNSON and JANE BUCKNER in partnership in KENTUCKY and the transactions of ROBERT JOHNSON my Attorney shall be as good and lawfull against me and my heirs as if I were personally to act myself, Given under my hand and seal this ninth day of October one thousand seven hundred and ninety four

PHIL: BUCKNER

At Albemarle October Court 1794
The foregoing Power of Attorney was produced into Court and acknowledged by PHILLIP BUCKNER, party thereto, and ordered to be recorded

Teste JOHN NICHOLAS, C. A. C.

pp. [On margin: NELSON to BERRY. Commission]
306- The Commonwealth of Virginia to [blank] Gentlemen of CHARLES CITY
307 County, Greeting. Whereas ROBERT NELSON and SUSAN his Wife by their certain Indenture of bargain and sale bearing date the ninth day of September one thousand seven hundred and ninety three have conveyed unto NICHOLAS BERRY of the County of Albemarle one certain tract of land containing fourteen hundred and forty three and half acres lying in County of Albemarle, and whereas the said SUSAN cannot conveniently travel to our County Court of Albemarle to make acknowledgment of the conveyance [the Commission for taking the acknowledgment and privy examination of SUSAN, Wife of ROBERT NELSON] Witness JOHN NICHOLAS, Clerk of our said Court the fourteenth day of March one thousand seven hundred and ninety four and in the 18th year of the Commonwealth

JOHN NICHOLAS C. A. C.

In Obediance to the above Commission to us directed, we WILLIAM ROYALL and SAMUEL DEMOVILL do hereby certify that we have this day personally examined the within mentioned SUSAN NELSON, Wife of the within mentioned ROBERT NELSON]the return of the execution of the privy examination of SUSAN NELSON] Given under our hands and seals this ninth day of May 1794

WILLIAM ROYALL
SAMUEL DEMOVILL

At Albemarle October Court 1794
The foregoing Commission and Certificate of the relinquishment of SUSANNAH NELSON's Dower in the lands cnveyed by ROBERT NELSON, her Husband, to NICHOLAS BERRY by Indenture bearing date the ninth day of September 1793 was returned to Court and ordered to be recorded

Teste JOHN NICHOLAS, C. A. C.

p, [On margin: NELSON to BLAINE, Commission
307 The Commonwealth of Virginia to WILLIAM ROYALL and SAMUEL DEMOVILL Genlemen of CHARLES CITY County, Greeting. Whereas ROBERT NELSON and SUSANNAH hihs Wife by their certain Indenture of bargain and sale bearing date the 16th day of November one thousand seven hun-

dred and ninety two have conveyed unto ISAAC BLAINE of the County of Albemarle one certain tract of land lying in County of Albemarle and containing two hundred and thirty nine acres and whereas SUSANNAH NELSON cannot conveniently travel to our County Court of Albemarle to make acknowledgment of the conveyance [the Commission for taking the acknowledgment and privy examination of SUSANNAH, Wife of ROBERT NELSON] Witness JOHN NICHOLAS Clerk of our said Court this 14th day of March 1794 and in the 18th year of the Commonwealth

JOHN NICHOLAS C. A. C.

In Obedience to the above Commission to us directed we WILLIAM ROYALL and SAMUEL DEMOVILL do hereby certify that this day we examined the within named SUSANNAH NELSON, Wife of ROBERT NELSON [the return of the execution of the privy examination of SUSANNAH NELSON] Given under our hands and seals the 3d day of May 1794

WILLIAM ROYALL
SAMUEL DEMOVILL

At Albemarle October Court 1794
The foregoing Commission and Certificate of the relinquishment of SUSANNAH NELSON's Dower in the lands conveyed by ROBERT NELSON, her Husband, to ISAAC BLAINE by Deed bearing date the 16th day of November 1792 was returned and ordered to be recorded

Teste JOHN NICHOLAS C. A. C.

p. [On margin: MELTON's Inspector's Bond]
308 KNOW ALL MEN by these presents that we HARWOOD BACON and EDWARD MOORE are held and firmly bound unto HENRY LEE, Esquire, Governor or Chief Magistrate of the State of Virginia and his successors in the sum of ten thousand pounds to be paid to the said Governor or his successors to which payment well and truly to be made we bind ourselves our heirs firmly by these presents; Sealed with our seals and dated this 11th day of September 1794

THE CONDITION of the above Obligation is such that whereas the above bound HARWOOD BACON is appointed Inspector of Tobacco in the Town of MELTON at the Warehouse in the said Town, Now if HARWOOD BACON shall well and truly demean himself in the Office of an Inspector and in all things do and act as the Law directs, then the above Obligation to be void or else to remain in full force and virtue

Teste ALEXANDER GARRETT HARWOOD BACON
EDWARD MOORE

p. [On margin: MELTON's Inspector's Bond]
308 KNOW ALL MEN by these presents that we JACOB OGLESBY and EDWARD MOORE are held and firmly bound unto HENRY LEE, Esquire Governor or Chief Magistrate of the State of Virginia and his successors in the sum of ten thousand pounds to be paid to the said Governor or his successors to which payment well and truly to be made we bind ourselves our heirs firmly by these presents, Sealed with our seals and dated the 11th day of September 1794

THE CONDITION of the above obligation is such that whereas the above bound JACOB OGLESBY is appointed Inspector of Tobacco in the Town of MELTON at the Warehouse in the said Town, Now if JACOB OGLESBY shall well and truly demean himself in the Office of an Inspector and in all things do and act as the Law

directs then the above Obligation to be void or else to remain in full force and virtue
Teste ALEXANDER GARRETT JACOB OGLESBY
EDWARD MOORE

p. [On margin: WAREEN Inspector's Bond]
308 KNOW ALL MEN by these presents that we SAMUEL SHELTON and SAMUEL DYER are held and firmly bound unto HENRY LEE, Governor or Chief Magistrate of the State of Virginia and his successors in the sum of ten thousand pounds to be paid to the said Governor or his successors to which payment well and truly to be made we bind ourselves our heirs firmly by these presents; Sealed with our seals and dated this 9th day of October 1794

THE CONDITION of the above Obligation is such that whereas the above bound SAMUEL SHELTON is appointed Insepctor of Tobacco in the Town of WARREN at the Warehouse in the said Town, Now if SAMUEL SHELTON shall well and truly demean himself in the Office of an Inspector and in all things do and act as the Law directs, then the above Obligation to be void or else to remain in full force and vertue
Teste ALEXANDER GARRETT SAMUEL SHELTON
SAMUEL DYER

p. [On margin: WARREN Inspector's Bond]
309 KNOW ALL MEN by these presents that we CLIFTON GARLAND and RICE GARLAND are held and firmly bound unto HENRY LEE, Esquire Governor or Chief Magistrate of the Sate of Virginia and his successors in the sum of ten thousand pounds to be paid to the said Governor or his successors to which payment well and truly to be made we bind ourselves our heirs firmly by these presents, Sealed with our seals and dated this 9th day of October 1794

THE CONDITION of the above Obligation is such that whereas CLIFTON GARLAND has been appointed Inspector of Tobacco in the Town of WARREN at the Warehouse in the said Town, Now if CLIFTON GARLAND shall well and truly demean himself in the Office of an Inspector and in all things do and act as the Law directs, then the above Obligation to be void or else to remain in full force and vertue
Teste ALEXANDER GARRETT CLIFTON GARLAND
RICE GARLAND

pp. [On margin: JONES to GRAY. Deed. Delivered with a Commission]
309- THIS INDENTURE made this [blank[day of December in the year of our Lord
310 one thousand seven hundred and ninety four, Between THOMAS JONES and MARTHA his Wife of County of Albemarle of the one part and FRANCIS GRAY of the County aforesaid of the other part; Witnesseth that THOMAS JONES and MARTHA his Wife for sundry good causes but more especially in consideration of the sum of a thousand pounds current money of Virginia to them in hand paid, the receipt whereof they do hereby acknowledge hath and by these presents doth bargain and sell unto FRANCIS GRAY and his heirs all that tract of land lying in the County of Albemarle and bounded; Begining at a red Oak saplin thence South thirty seven and an half degrees East one hundred and sixty poles to three Hiccories, a white Oak and Walnut in a Flat thence South twenty five degrees East ninety poles to a Chesnut Oak and Sasafras by the side of a Rock, thence South seventy degrees West

twenty nine poles to two white Oaks in a bottom, thence South sixteen degrees East three hndred and fifty eight poles to a Chesnut and Chesnut Oak on the side of the Mountain, thence North eighty degrees East fifty seven poles to a Hiccory on the side of a Mountain, thence South five degrees East ninety two poles to two Chesnuts on the West side of the Old Grant Line, thence North forty seven degrees West forty three poles to a Hiccory, thence North sixty five degrees West four hundred and ninety six poles to two Pines and a red Oak blazed, thence North twenty five degrees East one hundred and eighty poles to a Pine and white Oak, thence North twenty five degrees East three hundred poles to the first station containing by estimation eight hunded and eighty four acres be the same more or less together with all houses orchards profits and appurtenances thereunto belonging; To have and to hold the tract of land with its profits and emoluments hereby granted unto FRANCIS GRAY his heirs and we do forever warrant and defend the tract of land against all claims whatsoever, In Witness whereof the parties to these presents have fixed our hands and seals the day and year above written

Signed sealed and delivered in presence of

[no witnesses recorded] THOMAS JONES

At Albemarle December Court 1794

This Indenture was produced into Court and acknowledged by THOMAS JONES, party thereto, and ordered to be recorded

Teste JOHN NICHOLAS, C. A. C.

pp. [On margin: SANFORD to SANFORD, Power of Attorney]
310- TO ALL PERSONS to whom these presents shall come, whereas ROBERT
311 SANFORD the Elder now deceased did by his Last Will and Testament in writing in due form of Law made and now of Record in the Court of [blank] devise to his several Children equally to be divided among them certain lands lying in FLOYD's FORK in the County of [blank] and District [now State] of KENTUCKY as by a reference to the Commonwealth's Pattent for the same will more fully appear and whereas from the unsettled state of that County as well as the infancy of some of the Devisees of the said ROBERT SANFORD the Elder it has been found difficult if not impossible to secure the peaceable possession of the said lands and wheras from the operation of the Revenue Laws of the State of KENTUCKY imposing a Tax upon all lands lying within the State which Tax becomes payable in the year 1795 in default of payment thereof the landa are liable to be sold to raise the Revenues due thereon and it being expediant as well for the interest of the Children of ROBERT SANFORD the Elder still under age as the others who are of full age to take measures for the security of the said lands. NOW KNOW YE that we RICHARD SANFORD, REUBIN SANFORD, DURRETT SANFORD, JAMES BEASLEY and [blank] his Wife, one of the Daughters of ROBERT SANFORD the Elder, WILLIAM BURTON and SALLY his Wife, one of the Daughters and Devisees of ROBERT SANFORD the Elder, JOHN HEAD and NANCY his Wife, one of the Daughters and Devisees of ROBERT SANFORD the Elder and HENRY HEAD and ELIZABETH his Wife one of the Daughters and Devisees of ROBERT SANFORD the Elder in consideration of the Trust and confidence which we repose in our Brother, ROBERT SANFORD, the Younger, our true and lawfull Attorney for us and in our names [then there are several lines faded on the right side] agree that we will reimburse ROBERT

SANFORD the Younger which he may necessarily expend and we do hereby ratify and confirm whatsoever our Attorney shall do respecting the premises; In Witness whereof we have hereunto set our hands and affixed our seals the [blank] day of [blank] in the year of our Lord 1794 and in the Independenceof the United States of America the 19th.

RICHARD SANFORD
REUBIN SANFORD
DURRETT SANFORD
JAMES BEASLEY
WILLIAM BURTON
JOHN HEAD
HENRY HEAD

At Albemarle November Court 1794
The foregoing Power of Attorney was produced into Court and acknowledged by RICHARD SANFORD, REUBIN SANFORD, DURRETT SANFORD, WILLIAM BURTON, JOHN HEAD and HENRY HEAD six of the parties thereto and ordered to be recorded Teste JOHN NICHOLAS C.A. C.

p. [On margin: TWYMAN to TWYMAN, Power of Attorney]
312 TO ALL TO WHOM these presents may come, Greeting. Know ye that I SAMUEL TWYMAN of County of ORANGE in consideration of the special Trust and confidence which I have and place in my Brother, JAMES TWYMAN, that I have and by these presents do constitute and appoint the said JAMES my Lawful Attorney for me and in my name to sell or otherwise dispose of all or any part of my land in the State of KENTUCKY and execute such Deed or Deeds as may be necessary and that he may think proper which conveyance shall be as good and effectual as if done by myself in proper person and if there should be any claim set up by any person to any part of the lands, in that case to bring and defend suits as the case may be or compromise the same, and whereas JOHN CRAIG bound himself to survey some lands for me and failed to do the same, JAMES is hereby impowered to sue said CRAIG in my name for the recovery of the money and also for damages which I sustained in consequence of his failure, ratifying and confirming what my Attorney shall do in the premises shall be binding on me and my heirs, In Witness whereof I have hereunto set my hand and seal this 13th day of November 1794

SAMUEL TWYM,AN

At Albemarle November Court 1794
This Power of Attorney was produced into Court and acknowledged by SAMUEL TWYMAN, party thereto, and ordered to be recorded
Teste JOHN NICHOLAS, C A C

p. [On margin: WHITE to SANFORD, Power of Attorney]
313 KNOW ALL MEN by these presents that I JOHN WHITE of the County of Albemarle and in consideration of the trust and confidence which I repose in my Friend, ROBERT SANFORD, of the County aforesaid, have and by these presents do constitute and appoint ROBERT SANFORD my lawfull Attorney in my name and to my use to obtain from the Register of the Land Office of the State of KENTUCKY or from any other person or place authorized to grant it a Patent for a

Survey of the land lying in HARDIN County in the State of KENTUCKY it being part of JOHN WHITE's Entry of eight hundred and eight acres as by virtue of a Treasury Warrant No. 14963 on the North side of TURNER DICKSON's Survey of eight thousand acres as by a Plat of the survey made by JOHN HANDLEY and returned to the Office as may more fully appear and I do moreover appoint ROBERT SANFORD for the consideration [just too faded to make out more] whereof I have hereunto set my hand and affixed my seal this fifteenth day of November one thousand seven hundred and ninety four and in the nineteenth year of the Independence of the United State of America

JOHN WHITE

At Albemarle November Court 1794
The foregoing Letter of Attorney was produced into Court and acknowledged by JOHN WHITE, party thereto, and ordered to be recorded
Teste JOHN NICHOLAS C. A. C.

pp. [On margin: MOORE to DYER, Relinquishment]
314- Albemarle Sct. The Commonwealth of Virginia to SAMUEL MURRELL,
315 TANDY KEY and CHARLES WINGFIELD, JUNR. Gentlemen, greeting;

Whereas JAMES MOORE and ELIZABETH MOORE his Wife by their certain Indenture of bargain and sale bearing date the nineteenth day of November 179three have conveyed to SAMUEL DYER of the County of Albemarle one certain tract of land containing one hundred and fifty acres more or less lying in the County of Albemarle and whereas the said ELIZABETH cannot conveniently travel to our County Court of Albemarle to make acknowledgment of the conveyance [the Commission for taking the acknowledgment and privy examination of ELIZABETH Wife of JAMES MOORE], Witness JOHN NICHOLAS, Clerk of our said Court this fifteenth day of October 1794 and in the nineteenth year of the Commonwealth

JOHN NICHOLAS C. A. C.

In obedience to the within Order of the worshipfull Court of Albemarle to us directed, we met and examined the said ELIZABETH, Wife of JAMES MOORE privately and apart from her Husband [the return of the privy examination of ELIZABETH MOORE] Given under our hands and seals the 17th day of October 1794 and in the 19th year of the Commonwealth

TANDY KEY
CHARLES WINGFIELD, JUNR.

At Albemarle December Court 1794
This Commission and Certificate of the relinquishment of ELIZABETH MOORE's Dower in a certain tract of land conveyed by JAMES MOORE, her Husband, to SAMUEL DYER dated the 19th of November 1793 and were returned to Court and ordered to be recorded Teste JOHN NICHOLAS, C. A. C.

pp. [On margin: HENDERSON to MOORE, Relinquishment]
315- The Commonwealth of Virginia to SAMUEL MURRELL, TANDY KEY and
316 CHARLES WINGFIELD, JUNR. Gentlemen, Greeting Whereas JOHN

HENDERSON and FRANCES his Wife by their certain Indenture of bargain and sale bearing date the 22d day of September 1789 have conveyed to JAMES MOORE one certain tract of land containing one hundred and fifty acres and whereas the said FRANCES cannot conveniently travel to our Cournty Court of Albemarle to make acknowledgment of the conveyance [the Commission for taking the acknowledgment and privy examination of FRANCES, Wife of JOHN HENDERSON] Witness JOHN NICHOLAS, Clerk of our said Court the 13th day of October 1794 and in the nineteenth year of our Independence

JOHN NICHOLAS, C. A. C.

In Obedience to the within Order of the worshipfull Court of Albemarle to us directed we met and examined the said FRANCES, Wife of the said JOHN HENDERSON [the return of the execution of the privy examination of FRANCES HENDERSON] Given under our hands and seals this 17th day of October 1794 and in the 19th year of the Commonwealth

TANDY KEY
CHARLES WINGFIELD, JUNR.

At Albemarle December Court 1794
This Commission and Certificate of the relinquishment of FRANCES HENDERSON's Dower in a certain tract of land conveyed by JOHN HENDERSON, her Husband, to JAMES MOORE was returned to Court and ordered to be recorded

Teste JOHN NICOLAS, C. A. C.

pp. [On margin: SUTTON to LINDSAY, Deed]
316- THIS INDENTURE made this xiv day of November in the year of our Lord one
317 thousand seven hundred and ninety four, Between JOHN SUTTON of Albemarle County of the one part and REUBIN LINDSAY of said County of other part; Witnesseth that JOHN SUTTON in consideration of the sum of five hundred and fifty pounds current money of Virginia to him in hand paid do bargain and sell to REUBIN LINDSAY and his heirs one parcel of land in the County of Albemarle conaining by estimation seven hundred and five acres, it being the land that JOHN SUTTON now lives on and which he purchased a parcel of two hundred seventy acres of ROBERT LEWIS as by Deed bearing date the 17th day of May 1760 and recorded in the County Court of LOUISA and one other parcel of four hundred and fifty five acres of THOMAS WALKER as by Deed bearing date [faded] day of March 1767 and recorded in the County Court of Albemarle together with all its appurtenances, To have and to hold the parcel of land with its appurtenances to REUBIN LINDSAY and his heirs, and JOHN SUTTON for himself and his heirs unto REUBIN LINDSAY his heirs againt all persons whatsoever will for ever warrant and defend; In Witness whereof JOHN SUTTON hath hereunto subscribed his hand and affixed his seal the day and date above written

Signed sealed and delivered in presence of
SOLOMON TROWER,
MARSHALL DURRETT
THOMAS his mark X EDWARDS
JAMES LINDSAY

JOHN SUTTON
TEMPERANCE X SUTTON

Received of REUBIN LINDSAY the within mentioned consideration of five hundred and fifty pounds current money, Witness my hand and seal this 14th day of November 1794.

JOHN SUTTON

At Albemarle December Court 1794
This Indenture was produced into Court and acknowledged by JOHN SUTTON and TEMPERANCE his Wife, she being first privily examined as the Law directs, and

ordered to be recorded Teste JOHN NICHOLAS, C. A. C.

pp. [On margin: FLANAGAN to WOOD, Deed. Delivered to DRURY WOOD]
317- THIS INDENTURE made this first day of December one thousand seven
318 hundred and ninety four; Between JAMES FLANAGAN and PHEEBY FLANAGAN his Wife of the County of Albemarle of the one part and DRURY WOOD of the said County of the other part; Witnesseth that JAMES FLANAGAN and PHEEBY his Wife in consideration of the sum of one hundred and seventy four pounds, fifteen shillings current money of Virginia to them in hand paid by DRURY WOOD the receipt whereof JAMES FLANAGAN and PHEEBY his Wife doth hereby acknowledge, hath and by these presents doth bargin and sell unto DRURY WOOD and his heirs a certain parcel of land lying in County of Albemarle containing two hundred and thirty three acres be the same more or less and on the side of HALL's CREEK and bounded; [a few words readable on the left hand side, washed out on the right] thence on the said FLANAGAN's line South twenty nine degrees West thirty poles to a Gum, South sixty three and an half degrees West sixty nine poles to a Stake, thence South ten degrees West ninety poles to a Stump, thence seventy eight and an half degrees West two hundred and nineteen poles to a red Oak, thence North sixty four degrees East one hundred poles to a Post Oak, thence South sixty four and an half degrees East eighty two poles to a Gum, thence North fourteen degrees East forty six poles to the begining; together with all its appurtenances, To have and to hold the land with all its appurtenances thereunto beloning to DRURY WOOD and his heirs and JAMES FLANAGAN and his heirs the land with its appurtenances to DRURY WOOD his heirs against all persons will for ever warrant and defend by these presents; In Witness whereof we have hereunto subscribed our names and affixed our seals the day and year first above written
Signed sealed and delivered in presence of

[no witnesses recorded] JAMES FLANAGAN
FEIBY FLANAGAN

Received the first day of December on thousand seven hundred and ninety four the sum of one hundred seventy four pounds, fifteen shillings being in full for the within mentioned land as witness our hands and seals the day and year above written

JAMES FLANAGAN
FEIBY FLANAGAN

Memorandum: That on the first day of December one thousand seven hundred and ninety four that peaceably and quiet possession and seizin of the lands and premises within mentioned were had and taken by the within mentioned JAMES FLANGAN and by him delivered to the within mentioned DRURY WOOD and his heirs &c. according to the aforesaid intent and purposoe, as witness our hands and seals the day and year above written

JAMES FLANAGAN
FEIBY FLANAGAN

At Albemarle December Court 1794
This Indenture was produced into Court and acknowledged by JAMES FLANAGAN and FEIBY his Wife, she being first privily examined as the Law directs, and ordered to be recorded

Teste JOHN NICHOLAS, C. A. C.

pp. [On margin: MILLS to ESTELL, Deed]
318- THIS INDENTURE made this tenth day of July in the year of our Lord one
319 thousand seven hundred and ninety four; Between JOSEPH MILLS and MARY his Wife of County of Albemarle of one part and THOMAS ESTELL of said County of other part; Witnesseth that JOSEPH MILLS and MARY his Wife in consideration of sum of forty five pounds good and lawful money of Virginia to them in hand paid by THOMAS ESTELL the receipt whereof is hereby confessed and acknowledged, doth bargain and sell unto THOMAS ESTELL and his heirs one certain tract of land lying in County of Albemarle on the waters of LICKING HOLE CREEK and bounded by the lands of JAMES GILLUM, SAMUEL McCORD and JACOB BUSHANGE bounded, Begining at corner pointers to JACOB BUSHANGE's Fence South fifty degrees West one hundred and seventeen poles to pointers, thence North fifty degrees West two hundred twenty one poles to a red Oak, thence South sixty degrees East ninety poles to a red Oak, thence South seventy degrees East eighty poles to pointers, thence North fifty degrees East one hundred and sixteen pols to pointers, thence South forty three degrees Est one hundred and thirty three poles to the begining, To have and to hold the land with its appurtenances rents issues and profits thereof unto THOMAS ESTELL and his heirs and JOSEPH MILLS against the claim of any person will warrant and forever defend unto THOMAS ESTELL and his heirs, In Witness whereof I have hereunto set my hand and affixed my seal the day and year above written

Signed sealed and delivered in precence of

[no witnesses recorded] JOSEPH MILLS
MARY MILLS

At Albemarle December Court 1794
This Indenture was produced into Court and acknowledged by JOSEPH MILLS, party thereto, and ordered to be recorded
Teste JOHN NICHOLAS, C. A. C.

pp. [On margin: WHITE to MILLS Commission]
319- The Commonwealth of Virginia to JOHN GARLAND and JOHN STARKE
320 Gentlemen, Greeting; Whereas PHILLIP WHITE and LUCY his Wife of the County of HANOVER by their certain Indenture of bargain and sale bearing date the twenty fifth day of November seventeen hundred and ninety three have conveyed unto JOSEPH MILLS one certain tract of land lying in County of Albemarle containing three hundred and seventy acres and whereas the said LUCY WHITE cannot conveniently travel to our County Court of Albemarle to make acknowledgment of the conveyance [the Commission for taking the acknowledgment and privy examination of LUCY, the Wife of PHILLIP WHITE] Witness JOHN NICHOLAS, Clerk of our said Court, the fourteenth day of April seventeen hundred and ninety four in the eighteenth year of our Independence
JOHN NICHOLAS C. A. C.

HANOVER County, to wit
The within named LUCY WHITE did on this 26th day of November 1794 relinquish her right and title to the within land and premises contained in the Deed annexed in due form of Law. Given under our hands as Magistrates the day and date as aforesaid
JOHN GARLAND

JOHN STARKE

At Albemarle December Court 1794
This Commission and Certificate of Relinquishment of LUCY WHITE's Dower in a certain tract of land cnveyed by PHILLIP WHITE, her Husband, to JOSEPH MILLS was returned and ordered to be recorded

Teste JOHN NICHOLAS, C A C

pp. [On margin: TURNER to DAWSON, Deed]
320- THIS INDENTURE made the eighth day of October in the year of our Lord
325 * Christ one thousand seven hundred and ninety four; Between JAMES TURNER and REBEKAH TURNER his Wife of AMHERST County of one part and PLEASANT DAWSON of the same County of the other part; Witnesseth that JAMES TURNER with REBEKAH his Wife for the consideration of three hundred and seventy eight pounds, twelve shillings and six pence current money of Virginia to them in hand paid by PLEASANT DAWSON, I JAMES TURNER with REBEKAH my Wife hath bargained and sold unto PLEASANT DAWSON one certain tract of land lying in Albemarle County and containing by estimation six hundred and seventy one acres, Begining at a Pine and thence North thirty one degrees West six hundred and sixty four poles to a Pine on WILLIAM MOORE's and CHRISTOPHER HUDSON's pointers, thence North forty eight degrees West ninety two poles to a red Oak saplin in SAMUEL DYER's line, thence South forty six and an half degrees West forty poles to pointers on WILLIAM TOMPKINS's line, thence South forty five degrees East one hundred and seventy six poles to pointers on WILLIAM TOMPKINS, thence Southwestwardly with WILLIAM TOMKINS's line one hundred and sixty eight poles, thence South forty five degrees East one hundred and fifty two poles to a white Oak pointers on RICHARDSON HAMNER's line thence South twenty five degrees East sixteen poles to pointers, thence South fifty five degrees East one hundred and thirty poles to a white Oak, thence South twenty seven degrees East one hundred and twenty three poles to a Pine, thence South forty two and an half degrees East sixty nine poles to pointers in DAVID STRANGE's line thence North eighty six and an half degrees East one hundred and sixty poles to a Pine to the begining, Together with all houses and water courses contained in the tract of land and all the appurtenances belonging, To have and to hold the land and premises with all the appur-tenances unto PLEASANT DAWSON his heirs

* [This Indenture is completed on page 324 and 325 other material being on pages 322 and 323]

I JAMES TURNER do bind myself and my heirs to warrant and defend unto PLEASANT DAWSON his heirs from the lawfull claim of every person whatsoever; In Witness whereof we JAMES TURNER and REBEKAH my Wife hath hereunto set our hand and seals the day and year above written
Signed sealed and delivered in presence of

JOHN DAWSON — JAMES TURNER
JOHN E. FITSPATRICK
PETER LYON, SENR.
JOHN DAWSON

Received on the day of the date of the within Indenture of the within PLEASANT DAWSON the sum of three hundred and seventy eight pounds, twelve shillings and six pence current money of Virginia it being the full consideration the day within men-

tioned, I say received by me
Teste JOHN DAWSON, JAMES TURNER
JOHN E. FITSPATRICK
PETER LYON, SENR.
JOHN DAWSON

Memorandum; That on the day of the date of the within Indenture quiet and peaceable seizin and possession of the land and premises within mentioned with all the appurtenances was had and taken by JAMES TURNER and by him given and delivered to PLEASANT DAWSON according to the force form and effect of the within Deed; Witness my hand
Teste JOHN DAWSON JAMES TURNER
JOHN E. FITSPATRICK
PETER LYON, SENR.
JOHN DAWSON

At Albemarle December Court 1794
This Indenture was produced into Court by JAMES TURNER, one of the parties thereto, and ordered to be recorded
Teste JOHN NICHOLAS, C. A. C.

pp. [On margin: HARRIS's Writ]
322- The Commowealth of Virginia to the Sheriff of Albemarle County, Greeting.
323 You are hereby commanded to summon twelve good and lawfull men of your Bailiwick to appear on the lands of JAMES HARRIS near MOOR MAN's RIVER on the twenty second day of the present month at the place where JAMES HARRIS hath petitioned our County Court of Albemarle for leave to erect a Water Grist Mill to examine the lands above and below the property of others which may probably be overflowed and say to what damage it will be to the several proprietors and whether the mansion house of any such Proprietor or the Officer's gardens thereunto immediately belonging or orchards will be overflowed, to inquire whether and in what degree fish of passage or ordinary navigation will be obstructed, whether by any and by what means such obstructions may be prevented and whether in their opinion the health of the neighbours will be annoyed by the stagnation of the waters and also all other the conveniences and inconveniences that may arise to individuals in consequence of erecting the Mill which inquest so taken by virtue of this Writ signed and sealed by the Jurors due return make to the Justices of our County Court of Albemarle at the Courthouse on the second Thursday in December then next together with this Writ; Witness JOHN NICHOLAS, Clerk of our said Court, the eleventh day of October 1794 in the nineteenth year of our foundation
JOHN NICHOLAS, C. A. C.

In Obedience to a summons by virtue of a Writ ad quod damnum granted by the worshipfull Court of Albemarle directing the Sheriff of the said County to summon a Jury to meet on the 27th day of October in the year of our Lord one thousand seven hundred and ninety four to view a place on MOORMAN's RIVER opposite to JAMES HARRIS's Fence on which the said HARRIS intends to erect a Water Grist Mill, we of the Jury whose names are hereunto subscribed met agreeable to a summons for the purpose above mentioned and being first duly sworn on the Holy Evangelists of Almighty God proceeded to view the place intended for the erecting the said Mill, and do find that the said HARRIS owns the land on both sides of the River for some distance both above and below the said place where the said HARRIS intends to erect his Mill and do find that the lands of no other person will be damaged by erecting the said Mill and that neither the houses, gardens, orchards of any person will be overflowed nor will navigation be unduly obstructed nor the health of the neighbours damaged, Given under our hands and seals this 19th day of October 1794

[This entry is very faded especially on the right hand side. The names of the Jurors that are readable are} SAMUEL JAMISON NATHAN HARRIS JOHN DICKENSON
JOEL HARRIS THOMAS HARRIS WILLIAM MAUPIN
BARTELOT ELLIS

At Albemarle December Court 1794
This Writ of ad quod damnum together with the Inquest of the Jury taken by virtue thereof was returned to Court and ordered to be recorded
Teste JOHN NICHOLAS, C. A. C.

pp. [On margin: BUCKNER's Writ of ad quod damnum] [On the margin, "BUCKNER"
325- in the Text 'BROCKMAN"]
327 The Commonwealth of Virginia to the Sheriff of Albemarle County Greeting;

We command you to summon twelve good and lawful men of your Bailiwick to appear at the Courthouse on the second Thursday in December next at the place where WILLIAM BROCKMAN hath petitioned our County Court of Albemarle for leave to erect a Water Grist Mill, to examine the land above and below the property of others which may be overflowed and say to what damage it will be to the several proprietors and whether the mansion house of any such proprietor or the gardens thereunto immedately belonging or orchards will be overflowed, to inquire whether and in what degree fish of passage or ordinary navigation witll be obstructed whether by any and by what means such obstructions may be prevented and whether in their opinion the health of the neighbors will be annoyed by the stagnation of the waters and also all other the conveniences and inconveniences that may arise to individuals in consequence of erecting the Mill, which Inquest so taken by virtue of this Writ signed and sealed by the Jurors due return make to the Justices of our County Court of Albemarle at the Courthouse on the second Thursday in December then next together with this Writ, Witness JOHN NICHOLAS, Clerk of our said Court the eleventh day of October 1794 and in the nineteenth year of our foundaton
JOHN NICHOLAS, C. A. C.

In Obedience to a summons by virtue of a Writ of ad quod damnum granted by the worshipfull Court of Albemarle directing the Sheriff of the said County to summon a Jury to meet on the 6th day of December on the lands of WILLIAM BROCKMAN to view a place on PRIDDY's CREEK on which the said BROCKMAN hath erected a Water Grist Mill. We of the Jury whose names are hereunto subscribed met agreeable to a summons for the purpose above mentioned and being first sworn on the Holy Evangelists of Almighty God proceeded to view the place above and below where the Mill is erected and do find that the lands of WILLIAM DOWEL are damaged to the amount of seven pounds and the lands of THOMAS DOUGLAS are damaged to the amount of twelve pounds, eighteen shillings and nine pence and are of opinion that the acre whereon the Mill stands is worth ten shillings and are of opinion that no person or persons will be damaged below and that no person or persons's health will be annoied by the stagnation of the water and no obtruction of the passage of fish.

Given under our hands and seals the sixth day of December 1794

JAMES SIMS WILLIAM HAUL HENRY SHELTON
WILLIAM FLYNT JASON BOWCOCK MADISON BREEDLOVE
PETER FARGUSON JOHN MANSFIELD GRAVIT EDWARDS
RICHARD DOWEL JOHN DOWEL LAWRENCE FARGUSON

[In the middle of the page there is a drawing of WILLIAM BROCKMAN's land where the Mill is erected surveyed by JOHN D. GRIMES December the 6th 1794

Albemarle County, to wit

This day JOHN D. GRIMES appeared before me, JOHN KEY, a Justice of the Peace for the County of Albemarle and swears that he will well and truly survey and lay off one acre of land for a butment for WILLIAM BROCKMAN's Mill in the County of Albemarle agreeable to an Order of the said Court. Given under my hand the 6th day of November 1794

JOHN KEY

At Albemarle December Court 1794

This Writ of ad quod damnum together with the Inquest of the Jury taken by virtue thereof were returned to Court and ordered to be recorded

Teste JOHN NICHOLAS, C. A. C.

pp. [On margin: WERTINBAKER to CLUSEMAN, Deed]

327- THIS INDENTURE made this fourth day of December in the year of our Lord
328 one thousand seven hundred and ninety four; Between CHRISTIAN WERTINBAKER of the Town of CHARLOTTESVILLE and County of Albemarle of the one part and POLLY CLUSEMAN, PEGGY CLUSEMAN, MARIA CLUSEMAN and MICAJAH WASHINGTON CLUSEMAN all of the Town of CHARLOTTESVILLE and County of Albemarle of the other part; Witnesseth that CHRISTIAN WERTINBAKER in consideration of the sum of seventy pounds current money of Virginia to him in hand paid hath bargained and sold unto POLLY, PEGGY, MARIA and MICAJAH one certain lott of land containing half an acre in the Town of CHARLOTTESVILLE and distinguished in the Plan of the Town by the number Seventy One, To have and to hold the lott with its appurtenances unto the said POLLY, PEGGY, MARIA and MICAJAH to them their heirs and CHRISTIAN WERTINBAKER his heirs &c. the lott of land with its appurtenances unto POLLY, PEGGY, MARIA and MICAJAH and their heirs will warrant and defend. In Witness whereof CHRISTIAN WERTINBAKER hath hereunto set his hand and seal the day and year above written

Signed sealed and delivered in presence of

JOSEPH KENNEDY CHRISTIAN WERTINBAKER
CORNELIUS SCHENK

At Albemarle December Court 1794

This Indenture was produced into Court and acknowledged by CHRISTIAN WERTINBAKER, party thereto, and ordered to be recorded

Teste JOHN NICHOLAS, C. A. C.

pp. [On margin: POWERS to GARTH, Commission]

328- The Commonwealth of Virginia to JOHN GUERRANT, GIDIAN HATCHER
329 and THOMAS ROYSTER, Gentlemen, Greeting, Whereas WILLIAM POWER

and JUDITH his Wife of the County of GOOCHLAND by their certain Indenture of bargain and sale bearing date the 21st day of May seventeen hundred and ninety four, have conveyed unto THOMAS GARTH of the County of Albemarle one certain tract of land containing by estimation two hundred and fifty six acres and whereas the said JUDITH cannot conveniently travel to our County of Court of Albemarle to make acknowledgment of the conveyance [the Commission for taking the acknowledgment and privy examination of JUDITH, Wife of WILLIAM POWER] Witness JOHN NICHOLAS Clerk of our said Court the 18th day of October seventeen hundred and ninety four and in the 19th year of our Independence

JOHN NICHOLAS, C. A. C.

GOOCHLAND County, sct.

We do hereby certify that did go to the within JUDITH POWERS and examined her privately and apart from her Husband, [the return of the execution of the privy examination of JUDITH POWERS] Given under our hands this 21st of November 1794

THOMAS ROYSTER
GIDIAN HATCHER

At Albemarle December Court 1794

This Commission and Certificate of the Relinquishment of JUDITH POWERS's Dower in a certain tract of land conveyed by WILLIAM POWERS, her Husband, to THOMAS GARTH, and returned to Court and ordered to be recorded

Teste JOHN NICHOLAS, C. A. C.

pp. [On margin: THOMPSON to GARTH, Deed. Delivered NELSON THOMPSON
329- with a Commission. Delivered Mr. GARTH]
330 THIS INDENTURE made this tenth day of December in the year of our Lord one thousand seven hundred and ninety four, Between NELSON THOMPSON and SARAH his Wife of the County of Albemarle of the one part and THOMAS GARTH, SENR. of the same County of the other part; Witnesseth that NELSON THOMPSON and SARAh his Wife in consideration of the sum of three hundred pounds to him in hand paid NELSON THOMPSON and SARAH his Wfe hath bargained and sold unto THOMAS GARTH SENR. one certain tract of land lying in County of Albemarle on IVY CREEK and its Branches containing two hundred and fifty acres and is bounded; Begining at a Hickory in a Branch on the Dividing Line between the lands of the abovesaid THOMAS GARTH SENR. [formerly CHARLES STATHAM's] and the said NELSON THOMSON, down the Branch two hundred and ninety five poles to IVY CREEK, forty poles to a Hickory, thence South eighty five degrees East sixty one poles to pointers, thence South thirty six degrees East twenty three poles to a Pine along the line which was once COCKORAM's, thence South forty five degees East seventy three poles to a red Oak, thence South sixty seven degrees East sixty two poles to a white Oak, thence South twenty one degrees East twenty nine poles to a red Oak, thence South fifty five and an half degrees East eighty three poles to a red Oak and Pine, a corner in the said GARTH's lands, and on the Dividing Line between said GARTH and NELSON THOMSON, thence South sixty two degrees West one hundred twenty one poles to a forked Spanish Oak sapling in the Dividing Line and so along the same according to the Surveyor's Platt making several little variations to the first station, To have and to hold the two hundred and fifty acres of land with the appurtenances thereunto belonging to THOMAS GARTH and

his heirs and NELSON THOMSON and SARAH his Wife for themselves and their heirs by these presents forever warrant and defend the two hundred and fifty acres of land with the appurtenances unto THOMAS GARTH SENR his heirs against the claim or demand of any person; In Witness whereof NELSON THOMSON and SARAH his Wife hath hereunto set and affixed their hands and seals the day and year above written
Signed sealed and delivered in presence of
[no witnesses recorded] NELSON THOMSON
At Albemarle December Court 1794
This Indenture was produced into Court and acknowledged by NELSON THOMSON party thereto and ordered to be recorded
Teste JOHN NICHOLAS C. A. C.

pp. [On margin; RODES & MARTIN to EMMERSON Deed]
330- THIS INDENTURE made the tenth day of November in the year of our Lord
331 one thousand seven hundred and ninety four Between CHARLES RODES SENR. of AMHERST County and JOHN MARTIN of Albemarle County of the one part; and ZACHARIAH EMMERSON of Albemarle County of the other part; Witnesseth that CHARLES RODES and JOHN MARTIN in consideration of the sum of one hundred and sixty pounds current money of Virginia to them in hand paid by ZACHARIAH EMMERSON the receipt whereof CHARLES RODES and JOHN MARTIN doth hereby acknowledge, have and by these presents doth bargain and sell unto ZACHARIAH EMMERSON and his heirs one certain tract of land containing two hundred acres more or less situate in County of Albemalre on the North Branches of MEACHUM's RIVER being part of a larger tract and is bounded, Begining at pointers on the line of CHARLES RODES and with his line South sisty three degrees East seventy poles to a corner on the Roaling Road, thence a new line due South twenty seven poles to a Pine, thence a new line on the top of a Ridge South sixty degrees East one hundred and fifty poles on the line of JOHN RODES, deceased, and with his line one hundred and fifty poles to a corner on a Fence, thence North twelve degrees West one hundred and seventy six poles to pointers, thence South eighty five degrees West two hundred and thirty two poles to the begining; To have and to hold the land and premises with its appurtenances unto ZACHARIAH EMMERSON his heirs and CHARLES RODES and JOHN MARTIN for themselves and their heirs unto ZACHARIAH EMMERSON and his heirs the tract of land with its appurenances against the claim of every person will warrant and forever defend by these presents; in Witness whereof they have hereunto set their hands and affixed their seals the day and year above written
Signed sealed and delivered in the presence of
CLIFTON RODES, CHARLES his mark + RODES
JAMES ANDERSON JOHN MARTIN
LAWRENCE his mark X FITZGERALD
HENRY EMMERSON
At Albemarle December Court 1794
This Indenture was presented into Court and proved by the Oaths of CLIFTON RODES, LAWRENCE FITZGERALD and HENRY EMMERSON, three of the witnesses thereto, and ordered to be recorded Teste JOHN NICHOLAS, C. A. C

p. [On margin: CARR to NICHOLAS, Deed]
332 THIS INDENTURE made this Eleventh day of December one thousand seven hundred and ninety four; Between THOMAS CARR and LUCY his Wife of the County of Albemarle of the one part and WILSON CARY NICHOLAS of the same County of the other part; Witnesseth that THOMAS CARR in consideration of the sum of three thousand four hundred pounds current money of Virginia to him in hand paid hath bargained and sold unto WILSON CARY NICHOLAS a certain tract of land containing by estimation one thousand and fifty acres more or less lying in Albemarle County on both sides of the RIVANNA RIVER and bounded by the lands held by GARLAND CARR, SAMUEL CARR, PHILLIP BUCKNER, ALEXANDER CALVING and MARTIN HAWKINS with its appurtenances, To have and to hold the tract of land with its appurtenances to WILSON CARY NICHOLAS and his heirs and THOMAS CARR and LUCY his Wife doth covenant with WILSON CARY NICHOLAS and his heirs that they the tract of land with appurtenances to WILSON CARY NICHOLAS and his heirs will warrant and for ever defend by these presents; In Witness whereof THOMAS CARR and LUCY his Wife have hereunto set their hands and seals the day and year above written
Signed sealed and delivered in presence of
[no witnesses recorded] THOMAS CARR
LUCY CARR

At Albemarle December Court 1794
This Indenture was produced into Court and acknowledged by THOMAS CARR, party thereto, and ordered to be recorded
Teste JOHN NICHOLAS C. A. C.

pp, [On margin: NICHOLAS to JOUETT, Power of Attorney]
332-
333 KNOW ALL MEN by these presents that I WILSON CARY NICHOLAS do hereby constitute and appoint my Friend, ROBERT JOUETT of the County of Albemarle my lawful Attorney for me and in my name to purchsse a tract of land belonging to THOMAS CARR in the County of Albemarle hereby authorizing and impowering ROBERT JOUETT to bind me in any manner he may think proper for the purchase of the same in the same manner as if I myself were present and contracted therfore, hereby ratifying and confirming whaever my Attorney may do touching the premises, Witness my hand and seal this 12th dy of November 1794
Teste HUDSON MARTIN WILSON CARY NICHOLAS

At Albemarle December Court 1794
This Power of Attorney was produced into Court and proved by the Oath of HUDSON MARTIN, witness thereto, and ordered to be recorded
Teste JOHN NICHOLAS, C A C

pp. [On margin; NICHOLAS to CARR, Deed]
333-
335 THIS INDENTURE made this [faded] December in the year of our Lord one thousand seven hundred and ninety four; Between WILSON CARY NICHOLAS of the County of Albemarle of the one part and THOMAS CARR of the said County of the other part; Whereas WILSON CARY NICHOLAS hath this day purchased of THOMAS CARR a parcel of land lying in the County of Albemarle for the just and full sum of <u>three thousand five hundred pounds</u> to which is deferred to

the following days, to wit, the sum of three hundred and fifty seven pounds, two shilIngs and ten pence one farthing till the thirty first day of May one thousand seven hundred and ninety six, the sum of three hundred and fifty seven pounds, two shillings and ten pence one farthing till the thirty first day of May one thousand seven hundred and ninety seven; the sum of three hundred and fifty seven pounds, two shillings and ten pence one farthing till the thirty first day of May one thousand seven hundred and ninety eight, the sum of three hundred and fifty seven pounds two shillings and ten pence one farthing till the thirty first day of May one thousand seven hundred and ninety nine, and the sum of three hundred and fifty seven pounds, two shillings and ten pence one farthing till the thirty first day of May one thousand eight hundred, the sum of three hundred and fifty seven pounds, two shillings and ten pence one farthing till the thirty first day of May one thousand seven hundred and one, and the sum of three hundred and fifty seven pounds, two shillings and ten pence one farthing till the thirty first day of May one thousand eight hundred and two for which several sums WILSON CARY NICHOLAS doth execute his Bonds to THOMAS CARR for the securing the payment whereof. This Indenture Witnesseth that WILSON CARY NICHOLAS in consideration of the sum of five shillings by THOMAS CARR to him in hand paid, the receipt whereof WILSON CARY NICHOLAS doth hereby acknowledge and in consideration of the Debts aforesaid WILSON CARY NICHOLAS hath and by these presents doth bargain and sell unto THOMAS CARR his heirs all that tract of land conveyed by THOMAS CARR to WILSON CARY NICHOLAS by Indenture bearing date with these presents the boundaries of which land are expressed in the Indenture it being the same land whereon THOMAS CARR now resides, together with all and singular the appurtenances thereunto belonging, To have and to hold the premises with appurtenances unto THOMAS CARR and his heirs and WILSON CARY NICHOLAS his heirs unto THOMAS CARR his heirs against the claim of any person will warrant and defend, Provided always and these presents are upon this consideration that if WILSON CARY NICHOLAS his heirs shall well and truly pay or cause to be paid unto THOMAS CARR his heirs the full and just sum of two thousand five hundred pounds together with Interest accruing then these presents and every thing therein contained shall cease determine and become void or else shall remain in full force and virtue; In Witness whereof WILSON CARY NICHOLAS hath hereunto set his hand and seal the day and year first above written
Signed sealed and delivered in presence of
[no witnesses recorded] WILSON C. NICHOLAS
At Albemarle December Court 1794
This Indenture was produced into Court and acknowledged by ROBERTJOUETT, Attorney for WILSON CARY NICHOLAS, and ordered to be recorded
Teste JOHN NICHOLAS, C. A. C.

pp. [On margin: HOLT to SHELTON, Deed]
335- THIS INDENTURE made this [blank] day of December in the year of our Lord
337 one thousand seven hundred and ninety four, Between JOSEPH HOLT and MERIAH his Wife of County of Albemarle of one part and WILLIAM SHELTON of the same County of the other part; Witnesseth that in consdieration of the sum of one hundred eighty nine pounds JOSEPH HOLT and MERIAH his Wife hath bargained and sold unto WILLIAM SHELTON one certain tract of land lying in the

County of Albemarle containing two hundred and ten acres whereon JOSEPH HOLT now lives on the Southward side of the DS ROAD and bounded, Begining at a Pine Stump in ROGERS's line on the side of the Lane, then with the said ROGERS South fifty three West forty one poles to a white Oak near the mouth of the Lane, then South sixty three West one hundred and ten poles to a black Oak corner in BAILEY's land, then with the said BAILEY South forty two East sixty five and an half poles to a large white Oak on the side of a Branch, then East thirty four poles to a Stake in an Old Field, then South fifty seven East eighty two and a quarter poles to a Stake Oak on a Hill side, thence South twenty five East thirty one and three quarter poles to a small black Gum on the side of an Old Fence, thence North fifty three East one hundred and two poles to a Stump and Beeches on the side of ROAD's Fence also corner to LEWIS's land, thence with the said LEWIS's line North four West one hundred and ninety five poles to a small red Oak on the side of an Old Road in the said LEWIS's line also corner to WILLIAM ROGERS's land, then North eighty one West with ROGERS eighty eight poles to a red Oak on the side of the DS ROAD corner in said ROGERS's land, thence with the same South sixteen and a half West seventy poles to the begining; To have and to hold the two hundred and ten acres of land with its appurtenances thereunto belonging to WILLIAM SHELTON and his heirs and JOSEPH HOLT and MARIA his Wife for themselves and their heirs doth by these presents for ever warrant and defend the two hundred and ten acres of land with appurtenances unto WILLIAM SHELTON his heirs against the claim of all persons; In Witness whereof JOSEPH HOLT and MARIA his Wife hath hereunto set and affixed their hands and seals the day and year above written
In presence of

[no witnesses recorded] JOSEPH HOLT
MARIA HOLT

At Albemarle December Court 1794
This Indenture was produced into Court and acknowledged by JOSEPH HOLTand MARIA his Wife, she being first privily examined as the Law directs, and ordered to be recorded Teste JOHN NICHOLAS, C. A. C.

pp. [On margin: SEBREE to TERREL, Deed]
337- THIS INDENTURE made and done this nineteenth day of June one thousand
339 seven hundred and ninety four; Between JAMES SEBREE and MILLY his
Wife of County of Albemarle of one part and CHILES TERRELL of the same County of the other part; Witnesseth that JAMES SEBREE and MILLY his Wife for sundry good causes and considerations but more especially in consideration of the full and just sum of one hundred pounds current money to us in hand paid, the receipt whereof we do acknowledge hath and by these presents doth bargain and sell unto CHILES TERRELL his heirs all that tract of land lying in County of Albemarle and bounded, Begining at a Spanish Oak on a Path, thence North nineteen degrees East seventy six poles to two white Oaks, thence West twenty seven poles to a Poplar and dead red Oak, thence North thirty and an half degrees West ninety two poles to two white Oaks near TURKEY RUN, thence North thirty degrees East thirty six poles to a white Oak, thence North twenty degrees West sixty four poles to several saplins in THOMAS DOWEL's line, thence South sixty nine degrees West one hundred and eight poles to a small Oak in COLLINS's and COLEMAN's line from thence to the first

station containing by estimation ninety seven acres be the same more or less together with all houses orchards rents issues and profits thereof, To have and to hold the tract of land with appurtenances unto CHILES TERRELL and his heirs, and JAMES SEBREE and MILLY his Wife and their heirs the land and premises with the appurtenances unto CHILES TERRELL and his heirs against the claim of all persons will warrant and forever defend by these presents; In Witness whereof the parties to these presents have fixt their hands and seals the day and year above written
Signed sealed and delivered in presence of
JOHN D. GRYMES, JAMES SEEBREE
HENRY BROCK, MILLEY her mark X SEEBREE
ROBERT SANFORD
WILLIAM DICKENSON

Received of CHILES TERRELL the full and just sum of one hundred pounds current money of Virginia in full according to the form and effect of the within Deed this day and year within written
Teste JOHN D. GRYMES JAMES SEEBREE
HENRY BROCK MILLEY her mark X SEEBREE
ROBERT SANFORD
WILLIAM DICKENSON

At Albemarle December Court 1794
This Indenture was produced into Court and acknowledgedby JAMES SEEBREE, one of the parties thereto, and ordered to be recorded
Teste JOHN NICHOLAS, C A. C.

pp. [On margin: SIMMONDS to GIBSON, Deed]
339- THIS INDENTURE made between EPHRAIM SIMMONDS and FRANCES
340 his Wife of the one part and HENRY GIBSON of the other part; Witnesseth that EPHRAIM SIMMONDS and FRANCES his Wife in consideration of the sum of [faded] currency to them in hand paid, the receipt whereof is hereby acknowledged, hath and by these presents doth bargain and sell unto HENRY GIBSON and his heirs all that tract of land lying in County of Albemarle containing by estimation thirty nine acres and bounded, Begining at a white Oak [again the left hand side is readable but the right hand side is too faded] East twelve poles to a white Oak, thence North sixty degrees East one hundred and fifteen poles to pointers corner to DAVID MICHIE, thence along his line North thirty degrees West sixty six poles to the begining, To have and to hold the the right interest and claim of the land to HENRY GIBSON and his heirs and EPHRAIM SIMMONDS and his Wife hereby relinquish all claim to the land unto HENRY GIBSON his heirs &c., and EPHRAIM SIMMONDS for himself and his heirs the land and premises unto HENRY GIBSON his heirs against the claim of any person will warrant and forever defend by these presents, In Testimony whereof EPHRAIN SIMMONDS and FRANCES his Wife have hereunto set their hands and seals this [blank] day of December one thousand seven hundred and ninety four
Signed sealed and delivered in the presence of
[no witnesses recorded] EPHRAIM his mark X SIMMONDS

At Albemarle December Court 1794
This Indenture was produced into Court and acknowledged by EPHRAIM SIM-

MONDS, one of the parties thereto, and ordered to be recorded
Teste JOHN NICHOLAS, C. A. C.

pp. [On margin: PRICE to BACON, Deed
340- KNOW ALL PERSONS whom these may come that I RICHARD PRICE of
341 Albemarle County in consideration of the sum of fifty pounds current money of Virginia to me in hand paid by WILLIAM BACON of AMHERST County the receipt whereof I RICHARD PRICE doth hereby acknowledge, and by these presents doth bargain and sell unto WILLIAM BACON his heirs one Negro girl by the name of Sealy, To have and to hold the bargained and sold Negro unto WILLIAM BACON his heirs and I RICHARD PRICE for myself my heirs the Negro girl, Sealy, unto WILLIAM BACON and assigns against all persons whatever shall warrant and forever defend by these presents, In Witness whereof I the said RICHARD PRICE have hereunto set my hand and affixed my seal this fourteenth day of July in the year of our Lord one thousand seven hundred and ninety four
Signed sealed and delivered in presence of

HARWOOD BACON, RICHARD PRICE
RICHARD POWELL,
JACOB OGLESBY

At Albemarle December Court 1794
This Bill of Sale was produced into Court and proved by the Oaths of HARWOOD BACON and JACOB OGLESBY, two of the witnesses thereto and ordered to be recorded Teste JOHN NICHOLAS, C. A. C.

pp. [On margin: HARVIE to GOODMAN, Deed]
341- THIS INDENTURE made this tenth day of October in the year of our Lord
343 one thousand seven hundred and ninety four; Between JOHN HARVIE of the City of RICHMOND and MARGARET his Wife of the one part and CHARLES GOODMAN of the County of Albemarle of the other part; Witnesseth that JOHN HARVIE in exchange for other lands and in consideration of the sum of five shillings to him in hand paid, the receipt whereof he doth hereby acknowledge, hath and by these presents doth bargain and sell unto CHARLES GOODMAN his heirs the two following tracts of land lying in County of Albemarle and on the waters of IVY CREEK, the first consisisting of eleven acres and bounded, Begiining at a Pine in what is called ROBINSON's line, thence with said line North six degrees East thirty nine poles to a Post Oak in CHARLES GOODMAN's line, North sixty five degrees West forty two poles to a Pine Stump in said GOODMAN's Fence, thence South twenty degrees West thirty nine poles to a Post and red Oak to the line of an Old Field thence South seventy and an half degrees East fifty poles to the begining, the other tract consisting of one hundred and fourteen acres and bounded; Begining at a Poplar corner of said GOODMAN thence North seventy and one half degrees West ninety poles to a white Oak thence North twenty one degrees East two hundred and one poles to two Dogwoods in a hollow, thence South sixty five degrees East ninety three poles to a Stump in HORSLEY GOODMAN's Field, thence North twenty one degrees West one hundred and ninety nine poles to the begining, To have and to hold the two tracts of land unto CHARLES GOODMAN and his heirs, and JOHN HARVIE for himself and his heirs doth covenant with CHARLES GOODMAN and his heirs that

he will warrant and defend the title to the tracts of land with their appurteeances to CHARLES GOODMAN and his heirs against the claim or demand of any person; In Witness whereof JOHN HARVIE and MARGARET his Wife have hereunto set their hands and seals the day and year first above written

Signed sealed and delivered in presence of

JOHN SLAUGHTER — JOHN HARVIE
JOHN SNEED — MARGARET HARVIE
SARAH SNEED,
ROWLAND GOODMAN

At Albemarle December Court 1794

This Indenture was produced into Court and proved by the Oaths of JOHN SLAUGHTER, JOHN SNEED and ROWLAND GOODMAN, three of the witnesses thereto, and ordered to be recorded

Teste JOHN NICHOLAS, C. A. C.

pp. [On margin: GOODMAN to HARVIE, Deed]
343- THIS INDENTURE made this tenth day of October in the year of our Lord one
344 thousand seven hundred and ninety four; Between CHARLES GOODMAN and ELIZABETH his Wife of the County of Albemarle of one part and JOHN HARVIE of the City of RICHMOND of the other part; Witnesseth that in exchange for other lands and in consideration of the sum of five shillings to him in hand paid, the receipt whereof he doth hereby acknowledge, hath and by these presents doth bargain and sell unto JOHN HARVIE his heirs a tract of land lying in the County of Albemarle on the waters of IVY CREEK containing one hundred and twenty five acres and bounded; Begning at [faded] field, thence North twenty degrees East forty eight poles and [faded] poles to a post and red Oak Bushes [faded] North seventy and an half degrees West four hundred and fourteen poles to a Pine, thence South twenty one degrees West forty eight and an half poles to a white Oak, thence South seventy and an half degrees East four hundred and fourteen poles to the begining; To have and to hold the tract of land unto JOHN HARVIE and his heirs and CHARLES GOODMAN for himself and his heirs doth covenant and agree to and with JOHN HARVIE and his heirs that he will warrant and defend the title to the tract of land with their appurtenances unto JOHN HARVIE and his heirs against the claim ad demand of every person In Witness whereof CHARLES GOODMAN and his Wife have hereunto set their hands and seals the day and year above written

Signed sealed and delivered in presence of

JOHN SLAUGHTER, — CHARLES GOODMAN
JOHN SNEED — ELIZABETH her mark X GOODMAN
SARAH SNEED,
ROWLAND GOODMAN

At Albemarle December Court 1794

This Indenture was produced into Court and acknowledged by CHARLES GOODMAN, party thereto, and ordered to be recorded

Teste JOHN NICHOLAS C. A. C.

pp. [On margin: WERTINBAKER to BURCH, Deed]
344- THIS INDENTURE made this fifth day of December in the year of our Lord
345 one thousand seven hundred and ninety four; Between CHRISTIAN WERTINBAKER of the Town of CHARLOTTESVILLE of the one part and SAMUEL BURCH of the same Town of the other part; Witnesseth that CHRISTIAN WERTINBAKER in consideration of the sum of nine pounds current money of Virginia to him in hand paid hath bargained and sold unto SAMUEL BURCH one certain lot of land lying in theTown of CHARLOTTESVILLE distinguished in the map of the Town by the number four [4], To have and to hold the lot with its appurtenances unto SAMUEL BURCH and his heirs and CHRISTIAN WERTINBAKER for himself and his heirs unto SAMUEL BURCH his heirs the lot of land with its appurtenances will for ever warrant and defend, In Witness whereof the said CHRISTIAN hath hereunto set his hand and seal the day and year above written

Signed sealed and delivered in presence of

RICHARD BURCH, CHRISTIAN W. BAKER
CORNELIUS SCHENK,
JESSE LEWIS

At Albemarle December Court 1794

This Indenture was produced into Court and acknowledged by CHRISTIAN WERTINBAKER, party thereto, and ordered to be recorded

Teste JOHN NICHOLAS C A. C.

pp. [On margin: BURNLEY to BURNLEY, Deed]
345- KNOW ALL MEN by these presents that I JAMES BURNLEY of the County
346 LOUISA for sundry good causes and considerations but more especially for and in consideration of the Paternal affection which I have and bear unto NICHOLAS BURNLEY of the County of Albemarle and for the sum of five shillings to me in hand paid by NICHOLAS BURNLEY the receipt whereof is hereby acknowledged hath given and granted the possession and seizin of a certain tract of land lying in the County of Albemarle on the waters of BEAVERDAM CREEK and the courses supposed to be, Begining at a corner stone in said JAMES BURNLEY's line, thence along said BURNLEY's line South forty seven degrees West two hundred and thirteen poles to a corner Stone, GEORGE WEST's corner, thence North fifty two and an half degrees West eighty five poles to a white Oak sapling at WEST's corner, thence North twelve degrees East one hundred and ninety nine poles to pointers, JOHN BURNLEY's corner, thence North forty six degrees East forty three poles to a red Oak sapling, thence South forty two and an half degrees East one hundred and seventy two poles to the begining; containing by estimation one hundred and ninety six acres be the same more or less with all and singular the appurtenances thereunto belonging To have and to hold the land in fee simple to NICHOLAS BURNLEY his heirs and JAMES BURNLEY for himself and his heirs the land will warrant and for ever defend by these presents. In Witness whereof I have hereunto set my hand and seal this [blank] day of [blank] in the year of our Lord one thousand seven hundred and ninety four

Signed sealed and delivered in presence of us

CHRISTIAN SAILER, JAMES BURNLEY
JOHN BURNLEY,

MARY BURNLEY,
ALEXANDER GARRETT

At Albemarle June Court 1794
This Indenture was produced into Court and proved by the Oaths of CHRISTIAN SAILER and JOHN BURNLEY, two of the witnesses thereto, And at December Court 1794, was further proved by the Oath of ALEXANDER GARRETT, a third witness thereto, and ordered to be recorded
Teste JOHN NICHOLAS, C. A. C.

pp. [On margin: MELTON's Trustees to MONROE, Deed]
347- THIS INDENTURE made this third day of October one thousand seven hun-
348 dred and ninety four; Between CHARLES L. LEWIS, WILLIAM CLARK, HOWELL LEWIS and EDWARD MOORE, a majority of the Trustees of the Town of MELTON by Act of Assembly of one part and JOSEPH JONES MONROE of the County of Albemarle of the other part; Witnesseth that CHARLES L. LEWIS, WILLIAM CLARK, HOWELL LEWIS and EDWARD MOORE by virtue of an Act of Assembly for establishing the Town of MELTON on the lands of BENNETT HARRISON in the County of Albemarle and in consideration of the sum of forty six pounds, ten shillings current money of Virginia to them in hand paid by JOSEPH JONES MONROE the receipt whereof they do hereby acknowledge have bargained and sold unto JOSEPH JONES MONROE a certain lot of land containing half an acre marked in the plan of the Town [faded] To have and to hold the lott of ground with all its appurtenances thereunto belonging to JOSEPH JONES MONROE his heirs and CHARLES L. LEWIS, WILLIAM CLARK, HOWELL LEWIS and EDWARD MOORE, Trustees as aforesaid, for themselves and their heirs against the claim of all persons will warrant and by these presents defend; In Witness whereof CHARLES L. LEWIS, WILLIAM CLARK, HOWELL LEWIS and EDWARD MOORE have hereunto set their hands and affixed their seals the day and year above written
Signed sealed and delivered in presence of

GEORGE BRUCE, CHARLES L. LEWIS
ROBERT SNELSON, WILLIAM CLARK
HENRY GAMBLE HOWELL LEWIS
EDWARD MOORE

At Albemarle January Court 1795
This Indenture was produced into Court and proved by the Oaths of GEORGE BRUCE, ROBERT SNELSON and HENRY GAMBLE, witnesses thereto, and ordered to be recorded Teste JOHN NICHOLAS, C. A. C.

pp. [On margin: UERRING to HEAD, Deed]
348- THIS INDENTURE made this eighth day of January one thousand seven
349 hundred and ninety five; Between GEORGE HERRING of County of Albemarle of one part and MARSHAL HEAD of the County of ORANGE of other part; Witnesseth that GEORGE HERRING in consideration of the sum of one hundred and ten pounds Virginia currency hath and by these presents doth bargain and sell unto MARSHAL HEAD his heirs a certain tract of land containing by estimation one hundred acres be the same more or less lying in County of Albemarle and bounded, Begining at a white Oak saplin on a Branch corner to JAMES HERRING, North five degrees East one hundred and seventy four poles to a small Hickory,

thence North twenty five degrees East ninety one poles to a Post Oak in the hollow of a Mountain, North eighty degrees West seventy one poles to a small black Oak on the side of the Mountain, South ten degrees West one hundred and eight poles to a blown up Maple in a Swamp, South fifteen degrees East thirty poles to a black Oak on the Old Road, South twenty two degrees West sixty poles to a blown up Pine corner to WILLIAM DOLTON, South thirty nine degrees East seventy eight poles to a small Poplar and an old Beech tree, North twenty seven degrees East twenty one poles to an Apple tree at a bank of stones, thence to the begining; To have and to hold the tract of land with its appurtenances unto MARSHAL HEAD his heirs and GEORGE HERRING for himself and his heirs the tract of land with its appurtenances unto MARSHAL HEAD his heirs against the claim of any person will warrant and for ever defend by these presents, In Witness whereof the parties have hereunto set their hands and seals the day and year above written
Signed sealed and delivered in presence of
[no witnesses recorded] GEORGE HERRING
At Albemarle January Court 1795
This Indenture was produced into Court and acknowledged by GEORGE HERRING, party thereto, and ordered to be recorded
Teste JOHN NICHOLAS, C. A. C.

pp. [On margin: WHITE to DEFOE, Bill of Sale]
349- THIS INDENTURE made this second day of January in the year of our Lord
350 one thousand seven hundred and ninety five; Between JOHN WHITE of the County of Albemarle of one part and BENJAMIN DEFOE of the same County of the other part; Witnesseth that JOHN WHITE in consideration of BENJAMIN DEFOE obliging himself to maintain JOHN WHITE in a warm comfortable and decent manner for and during his own and natural life with such cloathing, victuals &c. as said WHITE has been hitherto furnished with hath and by these presents doth bargain and sell unto BENJAMIN DEFOE one young Negroe woman named Amey about fourteen or fifteen years of age, together with one feather bed and furniture, To have and to hold the Negro woman and feather bed and furniture to BENJAMIN DEFOE his heirs and JOHN WHITE doth for himself and his heirs covenant with the said DEFOE that he will warrant and for ever defend the title of the Negroe woman, Amey, the feather bed and furniture against the claim of all persons. In Witness whereof JOHN WHITE hath hereunto set his hand and seal the day and year above written
Signed sealed and delivered in the presence of
EDWARD MOORE, JOHN WHITE
JOHN MANSFIELD
JOHN LANE
At Albemarle January Court 1795
This Bill of Sale was produced into Court and proved by the Oath of EDWARD MOORE and JOHN MANSFIELD, two of the witneses thereto, and ordered to be recorded Teste JOHN NICHOLAS, C. A. C.

pp. [On margin: BROWN to MAUPIN, Deed]
351- THIS INDENTURE made this tenth day of October in the year of our Lord
352 one thousand seven hundred and ninety four; Between JOHN BROWN of the County of Albemarle of the one part and GABRIEL MAUPIN of the said County of the other part; Witnesseth that JOHN BROWN in consideration of sum of fifty one pounds, two shillings and six pence lawful money of Virginia to him in hand paid by GABRIEL MAUPIN, the receipt whereof is hereby acknowledged, hath and by these presents doth bargain and sell unto GABRIEL MAUPIN and his heirs a certain tract of land lying in County of Albemarle and bounded by the lands of DAVID GALASBY, WILLIAM FRETWELL and JAMES LEWIS and the courses are as follows, Begining at a Corner Stump in GALASBY's line and runing North [faded] East one hundred and eighty two poles to pointers, thence North eighty seven degrees East one hundred seventy six poles to pointers, North sixteen degrees West one hundred poles to a Pine Stump, North seventy two degrees West thirty eight poles to a corner Pine, South forty degrees West twelve poles to a Maple, South five degrees West thirteen poles to a corner Oak at the Road, thence up the Road with the meanders of the Road to BERNICE BROWN's line, South twelve degrees West thirty four poles to a orner white Oak in BERNICE BROWN's line, South fifty nine degrees West one hundred and ninety two poles in GALASBY's line, South nineteen degrees West forty poles to the begining; containing by estimation one hundred and thirty four and three quarters acres be the same more or less with the Estate right title claim and demand of JOHN BROWN his heirs, To have and to hold the land and premises with appurtenances unto GABRIEL MAUPIN his heirs and JOHN BROWN against any person will warrant and for ever defend by these presents; In Witness whereof JOHN BROWN hath hereunto set his hand and seal the day and year above written
Signed sealed and delivered in presence of

THOMAS CARR, JUNR. JOHN BROWN
JOHN TAYLOR
JOSIAH WALTON

At Albemarle February Court 1795
This Indenture was produced into Court and acknowledged byJOHN BROWN, party thereto, and ordered to be recorded
Test JOHN NICHOLAS, C. A. C.

pp. [On margin: DENTON to MAUPIN, Deed]
353- THIS INDENTURE made and done this twenty 2 day of May one thousand
354 seven hundred and ninety three, Between WILLIAM DENTON and AGNESS DENTON his Wife of County of Albemarle of the one part and THOMAS MAUPIN of the County aforesaid of the other part; Witnesseth that WILLIAM DENTON and AGNESS his Wife for sundry good causes but more especialy in consideration of the sum of fifteen pounds current money of Virginia to him in hand paid the receipt whereof is hereby acknowledged, hath and by these presents doth bargain and sell unto THOMAS MAUPIN his heirs all the tract of land lying in County of Albemarle and bounded, Begining at a scrub Oak corner to WILLIAM CARR thence down the different meanders of the Old Road one hundred and twenty two poles to several saplin Pines corner to WILLIAM [faded] thence to the first station, containing by estimation forty three and a quarter acres be the same more or less, together

with all houses orchards and every of their appurtenances and the rents issues and profits thereof, To have and to hold the tract of land and premises with appurtenances unto THOMAS MAUPIN his heirs and WILLIAM DENTON his heirs will defend the tract of land against any claim that shall hereafter appear, In Witness the parties of these presents have fixt our hands and seals the day and year above written

Signed sealed and delivered in presence of

CHARLES GOODMAN, WILLIAM his mark + DENTON
JOHN LAIN, AGNESS her mark + DENTON
PATIENCE LAIN
JOSEPH GOODMAN
JOHN his mark + BEAVER

Received of THOMAS MAUPIN the full and just sum of fifteen pounds current money of Virginia in full satisfaction of the conditions mentioned in the within written Deed according to the form and effect of the said Deed by us

CHARLES GOODMAN WILLIAM his mark + DENTON
JOHN LAIN
JOHN BEAVER his mark
PATIENCE LAIN

At Albemarle June Court 1793

This Indenture was produced into Court and proved by the Oaths of CHARLES GOODMAN and JOSEPH GOODMAN two of the witnesses thereto as to the sealing and delivery by JOHN DENTON, And on the same day AGNESS DENTON, one of the parties thereto being first privately examined as the Law directs, made acknowledgment of the same, And at February Court 1795 was further proved by the Oath of JOHN BEAVER, a third witness thereto and ordered to be recorded

Teste JOHN NICHOLAS C. A. C.

pp. [On margin: HARRIS to HARRIS, Deed. Examined and delivered sixteenth
355- April 1798]
357 THIS INDENTURE made this third day of April one thousand seven hundred and ninety four; Between JOEL HARRIS and ANNA his Wife of the one part and JAMES HARRIS of the other part, both of the County of Albemarle, Witnesseth that JOEL HARRIS and ANNA his Wife in consideration of the sum of ninety pounds to them in hand paid, the receipt whereof they do hereby acknowledge, hath and by these presents doth bargain and sell unto JAMES HARRIS his heirs one certain tract of land containing by estimation one hundred and ninety five acres be the same more or less lying in the Couuty of Albemarle on both sides of MOREMAN RIVER and bounded; Begining at a Spruce Pine standing on the South side of the River runing thence North sixty degrees East seventy six poles crossing MOREMAN RIVER to pointers, North fifteen degrees West eighty one poles to a white Oak , West one hundred and fifty poles crossing the River to pointers, North forty four degrees West fifty seven poles to a white Oak, North twenty seven degrees East forty one poles to a Hiccory, North fourteen degrees West sixty three poles to a Hiccory, South thirty three degrees West one hundred fifty eight poles to pointers on AGNESS ALFORD's line, South forty six and an half degrees East sixty poles crossing the River to a corner, North ten and an half degrees East twenty poles to a Spanish Oak thence

new lines seventy degrees East eighty two poles to pointers on JOHN McCORD's line, South forty poles to a corner Chesnut, South seventy degrees East ninety poles to a corner Pine, South fifteen degrees East fifty three poles to a corner Stone, thence North eighty five degrees East twenty poles to a corner Cherry Tree, South ten degrees East nine poles to a corner Locust, North eighty and an half degrees East thirty six poles to a Pine, North seventy three poles to the first station; To have and to hold the tract of land with all and singular the appurtenances unto JAMES HARRIS his heirs without the hindrance of JOEL HARRIS and ANNA his Wife their heirs, In Witness whereof JOEL HARRIS and ANNA his Wife have hereunto set their hands and seals this third day of April one thousand seven hundred and ninety four
Signed sealed and delivered in presence of

THOMAS McCULLOCK — JOEL HARRIS
NICHOLAS BURNLEY, — ANNA her mark + HARRIS
JESSE MAUPIN
THOMAS MAUPIN

Memorandum: That on the day and date within written quiet and peaceable possession and seizin was had and taken by the within parties according to the true intent and meaning of this Indenture, Witness our hands the day and date within

Teste THOMAS McCULLOCK — JOEL HARRIS
NICHOLAS BURNLEY — ANNA her mark + HARRIS
JESSE MAUPIN
THOMAS MAUPIN

On the day of the date within received of JAMES HARRIS ninety pounds the whole of the consideration, I say received by me

Teste THOMAS McCULLOCK — JOEL HARRIS
NICHOLAS BURNLEY — ANNA her mark + HARRIS
JESSE MAUPIN
THOMAS MAUPIN

At Albemarle January Court 1795
This Indenture was presented into Court and acknowledged by JOEL HARRIS, party thereto, and ordered to be recorded
Teste JOHN NICHOLAS, C. A. C.

pp. [On margin: BATES to COCKE, Deed of Sale]
357- THIS INDENTURE made this twenty fourth day of July in the year of our
358 Lord one thousand seven hundred and ninety four; Between WILLIAM BATES of Albemarle County of one part and [the next ten or so lines are too faded to read but from what can be made out this Indenure is a Bill of Sale for several Negro slaves and no place else in the Indenture does the first name of "COCKE" appear, also there appears to be a condition that WILLIAM BATES is to build "COCKE" a dwelling house } and whereas the said COCKE has delivered granted and made over to the said BATES the said Negroes as a consideration for work that has been made and yet to be made and finished by the time above specifyed, Now the Intention of this Indenture is being to secure to the said COCKE in the advantage he shall receive from the said Agreement and the delivery of the said slaves, if therefore WILLIAM BATES shall have well and truly built and performed the work by he 1st day of April 1795 as will amount to the sum of two hundred pounds current money of Virginia which sum is a consideration for the said slaves and a further sum of one hundred and seventeen pounds, thirteen shillings

and three pence of like money on Account adjusted receipt whereof he doth hereby acknowledge then the whole of this Indenture to be void otherwise in full force and virtue, Given under my hand and seal the 24th day of July 1794
Teste BENJAMIN WEBB, WILLIAM BATES
GEORGE MOORE,
At Albemarle February Court 1795
This Indenture was produced into Court and proved by the Oath of BENJAMIN WEBB, one of the witnesses thereto, and ordered to be recorded
Teste JOHN NICHOLAS, C A C

pp. [On margin: CLARKE to SMITH Deed]
358- THIS INDENTURE made this 13th day of December in the year 1794 Be-
360 tween WILLIAM CLARKE of County of Albemarle of the one part and
THOMAS SMITH and FRANKEY his Wife of the Parish of South Farnham in the County of ESSEX of the other part; Witnesseth that WILLIAM CLARKE in consideration of the sum of two hundred pounds to him in hand paid the receipt whereof he doth hereby acknowledge, hath and by these presents doth bargain and sell unto THOMAS SMITH and FRANKEY his Wife during the term of the life of the said FRANKEY in Trust of land lying in the Parish of Fredericksville and County of Albemarle containing four hundred and five acres being a moiety or part of the land of which WILLIAM CLARKE [left hand side readable the right side faded] being for eight hundred and ten acres and bounded by the land of GEORGE GILMORE, JOSEPH [B], JOSEPH HOPKINS and THOMAS JOHNSON, To have and to hold to the said THOMAS SMITH and FRANKEY his Wife during the life of the said FRANKEY and WILLIAM CLARKE or his heirs will cause to be immediately built on the premises at the proper cost and charges of WILLIAM CLARKE or his heirs a dwelling house sufficient for the comfortable accommodation and residence of THOMAS SMITH and his family, In Testimony whereof the parties have hereunto set their hands and seals the day and year first above written
Sealed and delivered in the presence of
JAMES WEBB WILLIAM CLARKE
WILLIAM HOWARD,
WILLIAM [ ]
At Albemarle February Court 1795
This Indenture was produced into Court and acknowledged by WILLIAM CLARKE, party thereto, and ordered to be recorded
Teste JOHN NICHOLAS, C A C

pp. [On margin: DERIEUX to BELL &c., Deed]
360- THIS INDENTURE made this 12th day of January one thousand seven hun-
362 dred and ninety five; Between PETER DERIEUX of the one part and THO-
MAS BELL, ROBERT JOUETT and CORNELIUS SCHENK of the other part; Witnesseth that PETER DERIEUX in consideration of the sum of five shillings to im in hand paid hath and by these presents doth bargain and sell unto THOMAS BELL, ROBERT JOUETT and CORNELIUS SCHENK all the right interest and claim of PETER in and to a lot of land and houses in CHARLOTTESVILLE being the same wherein said PETER hath heretofore lived, together with a certain parcel of

land adjoining the said Town heretofore also in the occupaion of the said PETER, which two lotts of land contain by estimation one hundred and thirty two acres and an half as also one Negroe woman named Suck, one riding carriage or phaeton and a certain balance of money due to the said PETER from ROBERT CAMBLE, Merchant of RICHMOND on an Account of Bills of Exchange furnished to said ROBERT by the said PETER and also to receive the money due by the said PETER to SAMUEL LEWIS for which the lotts of land before mentioned were conveyed to the said PETER, To have and to hold the lands and property unto THOMAS BELL, ROBERT JOUETT and CORNELIUS SCHENK their heirs in Trust to and for the following purposes, to employ or alienate the same in such manner and to such purposes as they shall think proper and convey away the whole of the right interest and claim of the said PETER in the premises and the money arising from the sale or employment thereof to apply to the payment of what debts this day are justly due from the said PETER to THOMAS BELL and CORNELIUS SCHENK and lett to ISAAC [ ], MICAJAH CHILES, MATTHEW RHODES, GEORGE DIVERS, JAMES CARDIN, JOHN JOUETT and NICHOLAS LEWIS the Elder, who have alrrady signed an Instrument of Writing expressing their assent to resort to the Trust and PETER DERIEUX doth hereby covenant with THOMAS BELL, ROBERT JOUETT and CORNELIUS SCHENK that said PETER his heirs the premises to THOMAS, ROBERT and CORNELIUS and their heirs will for ever warrant and defend, In Witness whereof he hath hereunto set his hand and seal the day and year above written

WILLIAM LOVE PETER DERIEUX
ALEXANDER WATSON
RICHARD H. ALLEN

At Albemarle February Court 1795

This Indenture was produced into Court and proved by the Oaths of ALEXANDER WATSON and RICHARD H. ALLEN, two of the witnesses thereto, and ordered to be recorded Teste JOHN NICHOLAS, C A C

pp. [On margin: BAILEY to LOVE for BELL & BROWN, Bill of Sale]
362- THIS INDENTURE made this twenty first day of June in the year one thou-
364 sand seven hundred and ninety four; Between WILLIAM BAILEY of County of Albemarle of the first part, WILLIAM LOVE of the said County of the second part and BENJAMIN BROWN and THOMAS BELL of the said County of the third part, Witnesseth that in consideration of the sum of five shillings current money the receipt of which is hereby acknowledged WILLIAM BAILEY hath and by these presents doth bargain and sell unto WILLIAM LOVE one certain Negroe man slave named Darby, To have and to hold the Negro slave, Darby, to WILLIAM LOVE his heirs and WILLIAM BAILEY doth for himself and his heirs warrant and defend the said Darby to WILLIAM LOVE his heirs against the claim or any person, yet upon this special Trust confidence and condition that whereas WILLIAM BAILEY is indebted to BENJAMIN BROWN the sum of fifteen pounds, eight shillings as appears by his Bond bearing date the same as this Indenture and whereas WILLIAM BAILEY is indebted unto THOMAS BELL in the further sum of nineteen pounds, five shillings and ten pence as appears by WILLIAM BAILEY's Bond to THOMAS BELL bearing date the first day of March 1793, Now if WILLIAM BAILEY shall on or

before the 25th day of December next pay unto BENJAMIN BROWN the debt aforementioned and pay unto THOMAS BELL the debt aforementioned to be respectively due unto them with legal Interest thereon then this Indenture to be null and void otherwise WILLIAM LOVE his heirs &c. are hereby specially intrusted whenever thereunto requested by either BENJAMIN BROWN or THOMAS BELL to sell and dispose of the Negroe man slave, Darby, to pay unto THOMAS BELL and BENJAMIN BROWN the debts mentioned to be due them respectively with legal Interest thereon and the residue if there be any to WILLIAM BAILEY his heirs &c., In Witness whereof WILLIAM BAILEY hath hereunto set his hand and seal
In presence of
THOMAS J. PRICE WILLIAM BAILEY
JOHN BROWN
At Albemarle February Court 1795
This Indenture was produced into Court and proved by the Oaths of THOMAS J. PRICE and JOHN BROWN, witnesses thereto, and ordered to be recorded
Teste JOHN NICHOLAS C A C

pp. [On margin: SIMS to GRAY, Deed]
364- THIS INDENTURE made and done this thirty first day of January one
365 thousand seven hundred and ninety five; Between JAMES SIMS and
MILDRED his Wife of the County of Albemarle of one part and FRANCIS GRAY of County aforesaid of other part [Witnesseth] that JAMES SIMS and MILDRED his Wife for sundry good causes but more especially in consideration of the full and just sum of one pound good and lawful money of Virginia to us in hand paid the receipt whereof is hereby confessed and acknowledged, hath and by these presents doth bargain and sell unto FRANCIS GRAY his heirs all that tract of land lying in the County of Albemarle and bounded; Begining at a large dead red Oak in a Field, thence North seventy two degrees East twenty poles to two red Oaks and a dead Chesnut Oak on the spur of a Mountain thence South six degrees West thirty seven poles to a small hycory in the hollow of a Mountain, from thence to the first station, containing by estimation two acres be the same more or less together with all houses orchards profits and appurtenances thereunto belonging; To have and to hold the land with each of its profits and emoluments hereby granted with appurtenances unto FRANCIS GRAY and his heirs and JAMES SIMS for himself and his heirs the land and premises with appurtenances unto FRANCIS GRAY his heirs will warrant and for ever defend by these presents; In Witness whereof the parties of these presents have hereunto set their hands and seals the day and year above written
Signed sealed and delivered in presence of
ACHILLES DOUGLASS JAMES SIMS
JOHN D. GRYMES MILDRED SIMS
At Albemarle February Court 1795
This Indenture was produced into Court and acknowledged by JAMES SIMS, one of the parties thereto, and ordered to be recorded
Teste JOHN NICHOLAS C A C

pp. [On margin: LOTT to LEWIS, Deed]
365- THIS INDENTURE made the tenth day of October one thousand seven hun-
366 dred and eighty seven; Between JOHN LOTT of the County of Albemarle of the one part and CHARLES LILBURN LEWIS of said County of the other part; Witnesseth that JOHN LOTT in consideration of sum of fifty pounds to him in hand paid has this day bargained and sold unto CHARLES L. LEWIS one certain tract of land containing two hundred acres be the same more or less situate in County of Albemarle on the North side of the RIVANNA RIVER joining CHARLES L. LEWIS the Parish line, thence a new line between ROBERT SHARP JUNR. and JOHN LOTT to a black Gum on the Creek, then bounded by the Creek to a Dogwood and Ash near the mouth of a Branch, then down the Creek to the LEWIS's line, the above lands with all the appurtenances thereunto belonging JOHN LOTT and PHEBE LOTT the Wife of JOHN LOTT, for the above consideration above mentioned to them in hand paid by CHARLES L. LEWIS the receipt we do acknowledge doth warrant and will for ever defend a good and lawful right in fee simple to CHARLES L. LEWIS his heirs, and JOHN LOTT and PHEBE LOTT the Wife of JOHN LOTT, bind themselves their heirs according to the true intent and meaning of these writings in witness given under our hands and seals the day and year above written
Signed sealed and delivered in the presence of

JOHN HENDERSON — JOHN LOTT
JAMES NOLAN — JUDITH her mark LOTT
ISHAM LEWIS

At Albemarle December Court 1787
This Indenture was proved by the Oaths of JOHN HENDERSON and ISHAM LEWIS, two of the witnesses thereto, And at February Court 1795, was further proved by the Oath of JAMES NOLAN, a third witness thereto, and ordered to be recorded Teste JOHN NICHOLAS C. A. C.

pp. [On margin: HADEN to HARRISON, Commission. Delivered to HARRISON]
367- The Commonwealth of Virginia to CHARLES M. TALBOT and JOHN W.
368 GILBERT, Gentlemen Greeting. Whereas ANTHONY HADEN and ANNA his Wife of the County of CAMPBELL by their certain Indenture of bargain and sale bearing date the tenth day of December seventeen hundred and ninety three have conveyed unto JAMES HARRISON of the County of Albemarle one certain tract of land containing by estimation four hundred acres be the same or less and whereas the said ANNA HADEN cannot conveniently travel to our County Court of Albemarle to make acknowledgment of the conveyance [the Commission for taking the acknowledgment and privy examination of ANNA, Wife of ANTHONY HADEN] Witness JOHN NICHOLAS, Clerk of our said Court this 9th day of May 1794 and in the eighteenth year of our Independence

JOHN NICHOLAS C. A. C.

CAMPBELL County Sct. In obedience to the within Dedimus we two of the Justices of CAMPBELL County have examined the within named ANNA HADEN, Wife of the within mentioned ANTHONY HADEN, seperate and apart from her Husband [the return of the execution of the privy examination of ANNA HADEN] Given under our hands and seals the 10th day of November 1794

CHARLES M. TALBOT

JOHN W. GILBERT

At Albemarle February Court 1795
This Commission and Certificate of the relinquishment of ANNA HADEN's Dower to a certain tract of land conveyed by ANTHONY HADEN, her Husband, to JAMES HARRISON &c. was returned and ordered to be recorded
Teste JOHN NICHOLAS C A C

pp. [On margin: GRAY to SIMS, Deed]
368- THIS INDENTURE made and done this thirty first day of January one thou-
369 sand seven hundred and ninety five; Between FRANCIS GRAY and
ELINER his Wife of County of Albemarle of one part and JAMES SIMS of the County aforesaid of other part; [Witnesseth] that FRANCIS GRAY and ELINER his Wife for sundry good causes but more especially in consideration of the full and just sum of six pounds current money of Virginia to us in hand paid, the receipt whereof is hereby confessed and acknowledged hath and by these presents doth bargain and sell unto JAMES SIMS his heirs all that tract of land lying in the County of Albemarle and bounded; Begining at two hycorys and white Oak pointers, thence South nine degrees West twenty eight poles to a Dogwood and two Gums on the rim of a Mountain, thence South twenty degrees East one hundred and thirty six poles to a black Oak, thence South eighty degrees East twelve poles to three small Hiccorys on the side of a Mountain, from thence to the first station containing by estimation twelve acres be the same more or less together with all houses orchards profits and hereditaments to the same belonging; To have and to hold the tract of land with appurtenances unto JAMES SIMS and his heirs and FRANCIS GRAY doth forever warrant and defend the tract of land against all persons, In witness whereof we have hereunto set our hands and seals the day and year first above written
Signed sealed and delivered in presence of
ACHILLES DOUGLASS FRANCIS GRAY
JOHN D. GRYMES ELINER GRAY
At Albemarle February Court 1795
This Indenture was produced into Court and acknowledged by FRANCIS GRAY, one of the parties thereto, and ordered to be recorded
Teste JOHN NICHOLAS, C. A. C.

pp. [On margin: KNOWLES to McCALLOUGH. Delivered JAMES P. COCKE
370- 8th of August 1797]
371 THIS INDENTURE made the thirty first day of March in the year of our Lord
one thousand seven hundred and ninety five; Between JAMES KNOWLES of County of AUGUSTA of one part and JAMES McCALLOUGH of Albemarle County of the other part; Witnesseth that JAMES KNOWLES in consideration of the sum of eighty pounds current money of Virginia to him in hand paid by JAMES McCALLOUGH the receipt and payment whereof JAMES KNOWLES doth hereby acknowledge hath and by these presents doth bargain and sell unto JAMES McCALLOUGH and his heirs one certain tract of land containing one hundred forty eight and one half acres situate in County of Albemarle and is bounded or adjoining to the lands of FRANCIS DAVIS, LAWRENCE FITZGERRAL and JOHN WOOD and now in the possession of JAMES McCALLOUGH with all advantages to the land belonging;

and also the right claim and demand of JAMES KNOWLES in the same; To have and to hold the land and premises unto JAMES McCALLOUGH and his heirs and JAMES KNOWLES and his heirs will warrant and for ever defend by these presents, In Witness whereof JAMES KNOWLES hath hereunto set his hand and affixed his seal the day and year above written

JAMES his mark + KNOWLES

At Albemarle April Court 1795
This Indenture was presented into Court and acknowledged by JAMES KNOWLES, party thereto, and ordered to be recorded

Teste JOHN NICHOLAS C. A. C.

pp. [On margin: CRAIG to BALLARD, Commission]
371- The Commonwealth of Virginia to BERNARD BROWN and BEZALEEL
372 BROWN Gentlemen Greeting; Whereas JOHN CRAIG and CATHARINE his Wife by their certain Indenture of bargain and sale bearing date July 1791 hath conveyed unto JOHNSON BALLARD a certain tract of land containing by estimation four hundred acres and whereas the said CATHARINE cannot conveniently travel to our County Court of Albemarle to acknowledge the conveyance, [the Commission for taking the acknowledgment and privy examination of CATHARINE, Wife of JOHN CRAIG]. Witness JOHN NICHOLAS, Clerk of our said Court this 18th day of October 1794 and in the 19th year of our Independence

TesteJOHN NICHOLAS C. A. C.

Pursuant to the within Dedimus to us directed, we have proceeded to examine the within named CATHARINE CRAIG privately and apart from her Husband, [the return of the execution of the privy examinatioin of CATHARINE CRAIG] As Witnss our hands this 1st day of April 1795

BERNARD BROWN
BEZALEEL BROWN

At Albemarle April Court 1795
This Commission and Certificate of the relinquishment of CATHARINE CRAIG's Dower in a certain tract of land conveyed by JOHN CRAIG, her Husband, to JOHNSON BALLARD was returned to Court and ordered to be recorded

Teste JOHN NICHOLAS, C A. C..

pp. [On margin: SMITH to MONTGOMERY, Deed]
372- THIS INDENTURE made this [blank] in the year of our Lord one thousand
373 seven hundred and ninety five, Between THOMAS SMITH, Major, of County of Albemarle of one part and FRANCIS MONTGOMERY of the said County of the other part; Witnesseth that THOMAS SMITH, Major, in consideration of the sum of thirty pounds current money of Virginia to him in hand paid by FRANCIS MONTGOMERY the receipt whereof THOMAS SMITH, Major, doth hereby acknowledge hath and by these presents doth bargain and sell unto FRANCIS MONTGOMERY and his heirs one certain tract of land containing thirty acres more or less on the Branches of MITCHAMS RIVER lying in County of Albemarle and bounded, Begining at a crooked white Oak on BENJAMIN BURGHER's line from thence a straight line to a Stump on the above mentioned THOMAS SMITH, Major, line and bounded by FRANCIS MONTGOMERY and BENJAMIN BURGER's lands and now in the possession of FRANCIS MONTGOMERY with all appurtenances; To have and to

hold the tract of land and premises with the appurtenances unto FRANCIS MONTGOMERY and his heirs and THOMAS SMITH, Major, will warrant and for ever defend by these presents, In Witness whereof THOMAS SMITH, Major, hath hereunto set his hand and seal this 6th day of April one thousand seven hundred and ninety five

THOMAS SMITH
RACHEL SMITH

At Albemarle April Court 1795
This Indenture was produced into Court and acknowledged by THOMAS SMITH and RACHEL his Wife she being first privately examined as the Law directs, and ordered to be recorded Teste JOHN NICHOLAS, C A C

pp. [On margin: HAYS to MONTGOMERY, Deed]
373- THIS INDENTURE made in the year of our Lord one thousand seven hundred
374 and ninety five, Between WILLIAM HAYS of County of Albemarle of one part and FRANCIS MONTGOMERY of the County aforesaid of the other part, [Witnesseth] that WILLIAM HAYS in consideration of the sum of one hundred and fifty pounds current money of Virginia to him in hand paid by FRANCIS MONTGOMERY the receipt whereof WILLIAM HAYS doth hereby acknowledge, hath and by these presents doth bargain and sell unto FRANCIS MONTGOMERY and his heirs one certain tract of land containing one hundred and forty five acres more or less lying in County of Albemarle on the Branches of MITCHUM's RIVER and bounded adjoining to BENJAMIN BURGER, THOMAS SMITH, RICHARD RICHARDSON, RICHARD DOLLENS and the said FRANCIS MONTGOMERY's lands and now in the possession of FRANCIS MONTGOMERY with all advantages to the land and premises belonging, To have and to hold the land and premises with the appurtenances unto FRANCIS MONTGOMERY his heirs and WILLIAM HAYS and his heirs the land and premises above mentioned with the appurtenances to FRANCIS MONTGOMERY and his heirs against all persons will warrant and forever defend by these presents; In Witness whereof WILLIAM HAYS hath hereunto set his hand and seal this 6th day of April 1794

WILLIAM his mark + HAYS
CHANLEY HAYS

At Albemarle April Court 1795
This Indenture was produced into Court and acknowledged by WILLIAM HAYS and CHANLEY his Wife, she being first privately examined as the Law directs, and ordered to be recorded Teste JOHN NICHOLAS, C A C

pp. [On margin: KNOWLES to FISHER Deed]
375- THIS INDENTURE made the eighth day of January in the year of our Lord
376 one thousand seven hundred and ninety five, Between JAMES KNOWLES and JEAN his Wife of the County of Albemarle of one part and FREDERICK FISHER of AUGUSTA County of the other part; Witnesseth that JAMES KNOWLES and JEAN his Wife in consideration of the sum of one hundred and ninety seven pounds current money of Virginia to them in hand paid by FREDERICK FISHER, the receipt and payment whereof is hereby acknowledged, hath and by these presents doth bargain and sell unto FREDERICK FISHER his heirs one certain tract of land containing two hundred ninety six acres more or less lying in the

County of Albemarle and bounded by the lands of JOHN THOMSON, JOHN DILLER, JAMES [ ], and SAMUEL WOOD, deceased, together with all houses, orchards and appurtenances thereunto belonging, To have and to hold the tract of land with appurtenances unto FREDERICK FISHER his heirs and JAMES KNOWLES and MARY his Wife and their heirs will warrant and defend the land and premises with the appurtenances unto FREDERICK FISHER his heirs against any other person In Witness whereof JAMES KNOWLES and JANE his Wife have hereunto set their hands and affixed their seals the day and year above written
Signed sealed and delivered in presence of

JAMES ANDERSON, JAMES his mark + KNOWLES
JAMES WALLIS JANE her mark + KNOWLES
JOHN KNOWLES

At Albemarle April Court 1795
This Indenture was produced into Court and acknowledged by JAMES KNOWLES, party thereto, and ordered to be recorded
Teste JOHN NICHOLAS, C. A. C.

pp. [On margin: HARDIN to BELL, &c. Deed]
376- THIS INDENTURE made this 9th day of February in the year of our Lord
377 one thousand seven hundred and ninety five; Between GEORGE HARDIN of County of Albemarle of the one part and THOMAS BELL and STEPHEN HUGHES of the said County of the other part; Witnesseth that in consideration of the sum of thirty two pounds, six shillings current money of Virginia to him in hand paid by THOMAS BELL and STEPHEN HUGHES to GEORGE HARDIN, the receipt of which is hereby acknowledged, the said GEORGE hath and by these presents doth bargain sell and deliver to THOMAS BELL and STEPHEN HUGHES and to their heirs one lott of land lying in the County of Albemarle and Town of CHARLOTTESVILLE containing half an acre known in the plan of the Town by the number [No] being the same whereon the said GEORGE now lives and heretofore purchased of the said STEPHEN, together with all and singular the appurtenances unto THOMAS & STEPHEN to them and their heirs and the said GEORGE doth for himself his heirs forever warrant and defend the granted premises to THOMAS BELL and STEPHEN HUGHES and their heirs yet nevertheless and upon the condition hereinafter specifyed, that is to say, that whereas GEORGE HARDIN is indebted unto THOMAS BELL the sum of nine pounds twelve shillings and six pence as appears by the said GEORGE's Note bearing date the twelfth day of May 179four and commonly called a Penal Bill and whereas the said GEORGE is indebted unto the said STEPHEN HUGHES the sum of twenty two pounds, thirteen shillings and one penny being the balance of GEORGE HARDIN's Note to STEPHEN HUGHES and bearing date the 21st day of November 1793. Now if GEORGE HARDIN pays the two debts as abovesaid on or before the first day of May next then this Indenture to be of none effect but if not to remain in full force and virtue, In Testimony of all which the parties have hereunto put their hands and seals the day and year above written
Signed sealed and delivered in presence of

RICHARD H. ALLEN, STEPHEN HUGHES
THOMAS CARR, JUNR. THOMAS BELL
ALEXANDER WATSON

At Albemarle April Court 1795
This Indenture was produced into Court and proved by the Oaths of RICHARD H. ALLEN, THOMAS CARR, JUNR and ALEXANDER WATSON, witnesses thereto, and ordered to be recorded
Teste JOHN NICHOLAS C. A. C.

p. 378 [On margin: APPERSON to APPEERSON Deed]
THIS INDENTURE made the sixteenth day of October in the year of our Lord one thousand seven hundred and ninety four; Between DAVID APPERSON of the one part and CHARLES APPERSON of the other part; Witnesseth that DAVID APPERSON in consideration of the sum of twelve pounds current money of Virginia in hand paid, the receipt whereof the said DAVID doth hereby acknowledge, hath and by these presents doth bargain and sell unto CHARLES APPERSON and his heirs all his tract of land lying in County of Albemarle and bounded, Begining at RICHARD BRUCE's line adjoining the SICK MOUNTAIN, thence the said APPERSON's line to [an Ivy Hill] a Chesnut in his line, from thence to JOHN HALL's line, thence on HALL's line to a corner red Oak, thence on the said APPERSON's line to the begining, containing sixty six and an half acres; To have and to hold the land and premises unto CHARLES APPERSON and his heirs, In Witness where-of DAVID APPERSON hath hereunto set his hand and affixed his seal the day and year within wrtten
Signed sealed and delivered in the presence of
DAVID EPPERSON — DAVID his mark + EPPERSON
ELIZABETHH LANGFORD
MARY EPPERSON
JOHN HAINS
At Albemarle April Court 1795
This Indenture was produced into Court and proved by the Oaths of DAVID EPPERSON, ELIZABETH LANGFORD and MARY EPPERSON, three of the witnesses thereto, and ordered to be recorded
Teste JOHN NICHOLAS, C. A. C.

pp. 379-380 [On margin: HUGHES to HARDIN, Deed]
THIS INDENTURE made the sixth day of February Anno Domini one thousand seven hundred and ninety five; Between STEPHEN HUGHES of the one part and GEORGE HARDEN of the other, both of the County of Albemarle Witnesseth that STEPHEN HUGHES in consideration of the sum of forty pounds current money of Virginia to him in hand paid, the receipt whereof he doth hereby acknowledge hath and by these presents doth bargain and sell unto GEORGE HARDEN and his heirs a certain lott of land lying in the County of Albemarle and Town of CHARLOTTESVILLE containing half an acre and known in the Plan of the Town by No. [blank] being the same whereon STEPHEN HUGHES formerly lived, together with all and singular the appurtenances thereto belonging; To have and to hold the land and premises with appurtenances unto GEORGE HARDEN his heirs and STEPHEN HUGHES and his heirs the lott of land unto GEORGE HARDEN his heirs against the claim of every person will warrant and for ever defend by these presents; In Witness whereof STEPHEN HUGHES hath hereunto set his hand and

seal the day and year above written
Signed sealed and delivered in presence of

ALEXANDER WATSON STEPHEN HUGHES
RICHARD H. ALLEN,
JESSE DAVENPORT

At Albemarle April Court 1795
This Indenture was produced into Court and proved by the Oaths of RICHARD H. ALLEN, JESSE DAVENPORT and ALEXANDER WATSON, witnesses thereto, and ordered to be recorded

Teste JOHN NICHOLAS, C. A. C.

pp. [On margin: CROSTHWAIT to TOOTWEILER, Deed. Delivered to TOOTWY-
380- LER]
382 THIS INDENTURE made this seventeenth day of February in the year of our Lord one thousand seven hundred and ninety five; Between ISAAC CROSTHWAIT of County of Albemarle of one part and JOHN TOOTWEILER of the County of ROCKINGHAM of the other part; Witnesseth that ISAAC CROSTHWAIT in consideration of sum of one hundred pounds current money of Virginia to him in hand paid by JOHN TOOTWEILER the receipt whereof ISAAC CROSTHWAIT doth hereby acknowledge, hath and by these presents doth bargain and sell unto JOHN TOOTWEILER his heirs a certain tract of land containing one hundred acres situate lying and being in the County of Albemarke near the foot of the PINEY MOUNTAIN and bounded, Begining at two Pines on JOHN DOWEL's and WILLIAM HALL's line, thence with DOWEL's line to the foot of a Mountain to a Rock, corner on JOHN ELLIOT's line, thence along ELLIOT's line to a Rock and corner Pine on WILLIAM HALL's line, thence with HALL's line to the begining; together with all houses orchards and water courses thereunto belonging; To have and to hold the land and premises with all and singular the appurtenances unto JOHN TOOTWEILER his heirs and ISAAC CROSTHWAIT for himself and his heirs the lands and premises with appurtenances unto JOHN TOOTWEILER his heirs will for ever warrant and defend by these presents against all persons having a lawfull claim against the same; In Witness whereof ISAAC CROSTHWAIT hath hereunto set his hand and seal the day and year above written
Signed sealed and delivered in presence of

JOHN his mark ⊢ RIPPETOE ISAAC CROSTHWAIT
REUBIN SANFORD ELIZABETH CROSTHWAIT
JOHN KEISTER,
JOHN DOWEL, JUNIOR

At Albemarle April Court 1795
This Indenture was produced into Court and proved by the Oath of JOHN RIPPETOE, JOHN KEISTER and JOHN DOWELL JUNR. three of the witnesses thereto and ordered to be recorded

Teste JOHN NICHOLAS, C A C.

pp. [On margin: CROSTHWAIT to TOOTWEILER Deed. Delivered to
382- TOOTWYLDER]
384 THIS INDENTURE made this seventeenth day of February in the year of our

Lord one thousand seven hundred and ninety five; Between ISAAC CROSTHWAIT of County of Albemarle of one part and JOHN TOOTWEILER of County of ROCKINGHAM of the other part; Witnesseth that ISAAC CROSTHWAIT for sum of one hundred pounds current money of Virginia to him in hand paid by JOHN TOOTWEILER, the receipt whereof ISAAC CROSTHWAIT doth hereby acknowledge, hath and by these presents doth bargain and sell unto JOHN TOOTWEILER his heirs one certain tract of land containing one hundred and twenty acres lying in County of Ablmarle on the PINEY MOUNTAIN and near the Plantation of WILLIAM HALL and bounded; Begining at WILLIAM HALL's corner Pine thence new lines South twelve degrees West one hundred and thirty six poles to a white Oak, South twenty eight degrees West fifty two poles to a Hickory, South five degrees West twenty two poles to a red Oak, North seventy eight degrees East forty two poles to a Pine, North thirty seven degrees East twenty poles to a Pine, North forty nine degrees East forty two poles to a white Oak, North sixty three degrees East twenty four poles to a red Oak, North thirty eight degrees East ninety two poles to a red Oak saplin in WILLIAM HALL's line, thence on his line North sixty four degrees West two poles to his corner white Oak and three red Oak saplins on the East side of the Mountain, North twenty six poles to the begining; together with all houses orchards and appurtenances, To have and to hold the land and premises with appurtenances unto JOHN TOOTWEILER his heirs and ISAAC CROSTHWAIT and his heirs will warrant and defend the said land unto JOHN TOOTWEILER his heirs, In Witness whereof ISAAC CROSTHWAIT hath hereunto set his hand and affixed his seal the day and year above written

Signed sealed and delivered in the presence of

JOHN his mark / RIPPETOE
REUBIN SANFORD
JOHN KEISTER
JOHN DOWEL, JUNR.

ISAAC CROSTHWAIT
ELIZABETH CROSTHWAIT

At Albemarle April Court 1795

This Indenture was produced into Court and proved by the Oaths of JOHN RIPPETOE, JOHN KEISTER and JOHN DOWELL, JUNR. three of the witnesses thereto, and ordered to be recorded

Teste JOHN NICHOLAS, C A.C

pp. [On margin: NELSON to GARLAND Delivered to SAMUEL DYER January
384- 1798 to obtain Wife's relinquishment]
385 THIS INDENTURE made this twenty eighth day of August in the year of our Lord one thousand seven hundred and ninety four, Between ROBERT NELSON of HENRICO County of one part and JAMES GARLAND of County of Albemarle of the other part; Witnesseth that ROBERT NELSON in consideration of two hundred and thirty four pounds, five shillings and eleven pence current money of Virginia to him in hand paid by JAMES GARLAND, the receipt whereof he doth hereby acknowledge, doth bargain and sell unto JAMES GARLAND a certain quantity or parcel of land being in the County of Albemarle in the NORTH GARDEN called and known by the name of the HEAD of the CREEK PLANTATION containing by estimation six hundred acres be the same more or less lying near the head of one of the North Branches of HARDWARE RIVER and is bounded by the lines of NICHOLAS

BERRY, WILLIAM LANGFORD and the said JAMES GARLAND, and it being the whole of the land claimed by ROBERT NELSON from NICHOLAS BERRY's line to the head of the North Fork of HARDWARE RIVER with all and singular the appurtenances to the same belonging, To have and to hold the land and premises with appurtenances unto JAMES GARLAND his heirs and ROBERT NELSON doth for himself and his heirs warrant the tract of land to JAMES GARLAND his heirs in fee simple and that he will defend the said JAMES and his heirs against any person claiming under him, In Witness whereof I have hereunto affixed my seal and assigned my name this twenty eighth day of August one thousand seven hundred and ninety four

Signed sealed and delivered in presence of

R. GARLAND, ROBERT NELSON
JAMES CLARKSON
BENJAMIN DAWSON,
WILLIAM LANGFORD

At Albemarle December Court 1794

This Indenture was produced into Court and proved by the Oaths of R. GARLAND and WILLIAM LANGFORD, two of the witnesses thereto, And at April Court 1795, was further proved by the Oath of JAMES CLARKSON, a third witness thereto, and ordered to be recorded Teste JOHN NICHOLAS C. A. C.

pp. [On margin: WALKER to JONES, Deed]
386- THIS INDENTURE made this eighteenth day of May in the year of our Lord
387 one thousand seven hundred and ninety five, Between WILLIAM WALKER and ELIZABETH his Wife of the County of Albemarle of the one part and LAIN JONES of the aforesaid County of the other part; Whereas ORLANDO JONES by his Deed bearing date the twenty seventh day of November in the year one thousand seven hundred and seventy one did for certain considerations therein expressed covenant for himself and his heirs to stand seized and possessed of and in all the Plantation seat and tract of land situate in the County of Albemarle commonly called MOUNT GALLANT containing by estimation four hundred acres also of and in ten Negroe slaves known by the named following, vizt., Jacob, Matt, Phebe, Mary, Joe, Gabriel, Barsheb, David, Phill and Andrew with all their present and future increase to the use of ORLANDO JONES and ELIZABETH CLAYTON his then intended Wife during the coverture between them and if ELIZABETH should survive him then to the use and behoof of ELIZABETH for and during her natural life and from and after her decease to the use and behoof of the heirs of ORLANDO JONES and ELIZABETH between them lawfully begotten but if ORLANDO should survive ELIZABETH then to the use and behoof of ORLANDO for and during his natural life and from and after his decease then to the use and behoof of the heirs of the bodies of ORLANDO and ELIZAETH between them lawfully begotten as by the Deed of Covenant and Will more fully and at large appears and whereas the marriage between ORLANDO JONES and ELIZAETH CLAYTON did take effect and ORLANDO is since dead without out issue by ELIZABETH and ELIZABETH hath since intermarried with WILLIAM WALKER and WILLIAM WALKER and ELIZABETH his Wife have agreed to sell the premises in the said Deed of Covenant mentioned to LAIN JONES, who is the only Son of ORLANDO JONES by a former Wife

excepting the following slaves by the following names [to wit] Jacob. Barsheba, Betsey, Polly, Kate, Harry, John, Washington and Billy which WILLIAM WALKER and ELIZABETH his Wife do make a reserve of during the natural life of ELIZABETH,

NOW THIS INDENTURE WITNESSETH that in consideration of the sum of five hundred and seventy pounds current money of Virginia to them the said WILLIAM WALKER and ELIZABETH his Wife in hand paid by LAIN JONES the receipt whereof they do hereby acknowledge, WILLIAM WALKER and ELIZABETH his Wife have bargained sold and surrendered unto LAIN JONES the tract of land commonly called MOUNT GALLANT lying in the County of Albemarle and containing by estimation four hundred acres also the slaves of the following names [to wit] Joe, Phebe, Mary, Hannah, Kitty, Nancey, Gabriel, Jack, Venus, Martin, Patience, Mourning and the male child of Kitty's unnamed together with the future increase of the female slaves and also all the interest and right of ELIZABETH or the said WILLIAM under the Deed of Covenant, To have and to hold the premises hereby granted barganed sold and surrendered to LAIN JONE his heirs and WILLIAM WALKER and ELIZABETH his Wife shall and will warrant for themselves and their heirs the premises hereby granted sold and surrendered to LAIN JONES his heirs against the claim of any person lawfully claiming under them; In Witness whereof WILLIAM WALKER and ELIZABETH his Wife have hereunto set their hands and affixed their seals the day and year first above written

Signed sealed and delivered in presence of

JOSEPH COLEMAN, WILLIAM WALKER
GEORGE PERRY, ELIZABETH WALKER
NICHOLAS [ ]

At Albemarle June Court 1795

This Indenture was produced into Court and acknowledged by WILLIAM WALKER one of the parties thereto and ordered to be recorded

Teste JOHN NICHOLAS, C A C

pp. [On margin: NICHOLAS to SOLOMON &c., Deed]
388- THIS INDENTURE made this seventeenth day of February one thousand
389 seven hundred and ninety five; Between WILSON CARY NICHOLAS and MARGARET his Wife of the County of Albemarle of one part and ISRAEL COHEN and BENJAMIN SOLOMON of the other part; Witnesseth that WILSON CARY NICHOLAS and MARGARET his Wife in consideration of the full and just sum of twenty five pounds current money of Virginia to them in hand paid, the receipt whereof they do hereby acknowledge, hath and by these presents doth bargain and sell unto ISRAEL COHEN and BENJAMIN SOLOMON their heirs one half acre lott of land in the Town of WARREN adjoining the Warehouse Lott on one side and cross the street between the said Lott and NATHANIEL ANDERSON's lott on the other side and known by the name of THOMAS ANDERSON'sLott, together with all houses fences and water courses thereunto belonging, and the rens issues and profits thereof, To have and to hold the half acre lott of land with the appurtenances unto ISRAEL COHEN and BENJAMIN SOLOMON their heirs and WILSON CARY NICHOLAS and MARGARET his Wife and their heirs will warrant and defend against the claim of any person, In Witness whereof WILSON CARY NICHOLAS

and MARGARET his Wife have hereunto set their hands and affixed their seals the day and year above written
Signed sealed and delivered in presence of
JOHN STAPLES, WILSON CARY NICHOLAS
ALEXANDER GORDON
THOMAS C. FLETCHER
At Albemarle June Court 1795
This Indenture was produced into Court and acknowledged by WILSON CARY NICHOLAS, party thereto, and ordered to be recorded
Teste JOHN NICHOLAS C. A. C.

pp. [On margin; NICHOLAS to SOLOMON, Deed]
388- THIS INDENTURE made this twenty third day of February one thousand
389 seven hundred and ninety five; Between WILSON CARY NICHOLAS and MARGARET his Wife of the County of Albemarle of one part and BENJAMIN SOLOMON of the other part; Witnesseth that WILSON CARY NICHOLAS and MARGARET his Wife in consideration of the full and just sum of fifteen pounds current money of Virginia to them in hand paid, the receipt whereof is hereby acknowledged hath and by these presents doth bargain and sell unto BENJAMIN SOLOMON his heirs an half acre of land in the Town of WARREN number [blank] adjoining Capt. JOHN NAPIER's Lott and JOHN BURKS's Lott on the other side by the name of THOMAS BALLOW's Lott, together with all houses waters courses and ways thereto belonging and the rents issues and profits thereof, To have and to hold the land with the appurtenances unto BENJAMIN SOLOMON his heirs and WILSON CARY NICHOLAS and MARGARET his Wife the half acre lott of land and premises unto BENJAMIN SOLOMON his heirs shall warrant and for ever defend against the claim of every person; In Witness whereof we have hereunto set our hands and seals the day and year above written
Signed sealed and delivered in presence of
[no witnesses recorded] WILSON CARY NICHOLAS
At Albemarle June Court 1795
This Indenture was produced into Court and acknowledged by WILSON C. NICHOLAS, party thereto, and ordered to be recorded
Teste JOHN NICHOLAS, C A C

pp. [On margin: VERNON to DAVIS, Deed, Delivered Capt. ROBERT DAVIS]
389- THIS INDENTURE made this fourteenth day of March in the year of our Lord
390 one thousand seven hundred and ninety five; Between RICHARD VERNON of the County of MADISON of the one part and EDMUND DAVIS of County of Albemarle of the other part; Witnesseth that RICHARD VERNON in consideration of the sum of four hundred and thirty six Dollars in hand paid by EDMUND DAVIS, the receipt whereof RICHARD VERNON doth hereby acknowledge, hath and by these presents doth bargain and sell unto EDMUND DAVIS his heirs one certain tract of land lying in County of Albemarle on the head Branches of PINEY RUN containing by an original survey four hundred acres but by a late survey four hundred and thirty six acres and bounded, Begining at JOSEPH KEATON's corner two Pines with the addition of a white Oak, scrub Oak and red Oak pointers, thence South

thirty four degrees East three hundred and twenty two poles to pointers, thence South fifty six degrees West one hundred and ninety eight poles to a Hiccory on a Run, thence North thirty eight degrees West two hundred and twenty poles to JOSEPH MERIDITH's corner pointers but thought to be JOSEPH MORTON's land, thence with his line North one hundred and forty four poles to a Stake by a scrub Oak with the addition of two black Oak pointers in JAMES KEATON's line, thence in the said KEATON's line North sixty four degrees East one hundred and thirty nine poles to the first station; and RICHARD VERNON doth hereby warrant and defend the right and title of the land clear of all incumbrances and free from the claim of all persons with all appurtenances in fee simple unto EDMUND DAVIS his heirs, In Testimony whereof RICHARD VERNON hath hereunto set his hand and seal the day and year aforesaid

Signed sealed and delivered in presence of

R. BRUCE, RICHARD his mark + VERNON
THOMAS his mark STONE
ISAAC DAVIS, JUNR.
SAMUEL TWYMAN,
JAMES BARBOUR, JUNR.
JOSEPH SNELL

Memorandum: That RICHARD VERNON doth agree that any errors in the courses to the within Deed or any error therein of whatsoever nature shall be of no advantage to him but the said DAVIS shall have and enjoy all and singular the premises, In Witness whereof RICHARD VERNON hath hereunto set his hand and seal the day and year aforesaid

Teste R. BRUCE RICHARD his mark + VERNON
ISAAC DAVIS, JUNR.
THOMAS his mark + STONE
JAMES BARBOUR, JUNR.
SAMUEL TWYMAN,
Teste JOSEPH SNELL

At Albemarle June Court 1795

This Indenture was produced into Court and proved by the Oaths of RICHARD BRUCE, ISAAC DAVIS, JUNR and THOMAS STONE, three of the witnesses thereto, and ordered to be recorded

Teste JOHN NICHOLAS C.A.C.

pp. [On margin: BURNLEY to SAILER, Commission]
390- The Commonwealth of Virginia to NELSON ANDERSON and WILLIAM
391 PHILLIPS, Gentlemen, Greeting; Whereas JOHN BURNLEY and SUSANNAH his Wife of the County of LOUISA by their certain Indenture of bargain and sale bearing date the twelfth day of June 1794 have conveyed unto CHRISTIAN SAILER of the County of Albemarle one tract of land lying in the County of Albemarke containing one hundred and eighty two acres more or less, and whereas the said SUSANNAH cannot conveniently travel to our Court of Albemarle to make acknowledgment of the conveyance [the Commission for taking the acknowledgment and privy examination of SUSANNAH, Wife of JOHN BURNLEY] Witness JOHN NICHOLAS, Clerk of our Court, this tenth day of March 1795 and in the 19th year

of our Foundation

JOHN NICHOLAS, C A C

In Obedience to the honourable Court of Albemarle we have met at the house of JOHN BURNLEY and have proceeded to take the privy examination of MRS. SUSANNA BURNLEY seperately and apart from her Husband and she freely and voluntarily relinquishes her right of Dower, Given under our hands this ninth day of April 1795

NELSON ANDERSON
WILLIAM PHILLIPS

At Albemarle June Court 1795
This Commission of the Relinquishment of SUSANNAH BURNLEY's Dower was returned into Court and ordered to be recorded

Teste JOHN NICHOLAS, C A C

pp. [On margin: SIMMONDS to McCLARY, Deed of Trust]
391- THIS INDENTURE made on the twenty fifth day of October in the year of
392 Christ one thousand seven hundred and ninety four; Between EPHRAIM SIMMONDS and MARY his Wife of the one part and JOHN McCLARY of the other part; Witnesseth that in consideratin of the sum of one hundred and ten pounds two shillings current money of Virginia which EPHRAIM SIMMONDS and MARY his Wife are justly indebted to JOHN McCLARY and honestly desire to secure and pay to him and in further consideration of the sum of five shillings of like money to EPHRAIM SIMMONDS and MARY his Wife in hand paid by JOHN McCLARY the receipt whereof they do acknowledge, hath and by these presents doth bargain and sell unto JOHN McCLARY and his heirs one certain tract of land lying in County of Albemarle whereon EPHRAIM SIMMONDS and MARY his Wife at present live containing by estimation three hundred and forty three acres be the same more or less which land was purchased by EPHRAIM SIMMONDS of a certain FROST & SNOW, also seven Negroes [to wit] Minney, Manuel, Ivie, Hannah, Poll and Hannah's two youngest Children, Nan and Joe, with all the appurtenances thereunto belonging, To have and to hold the land slaves and premises unto JOHN McCLARY his heirs against EPHRAIM SIMMONDS and MARY his Wife their heirs upon Trust nevertheless the said JOHN McCLARY his heirs after the first day of November next ensuing or as soon as JOHN McCLARY his heirs shall think proper or at the request of EPHRAIM SIMMONDS [which ever of the two circumsances first happens] shall sell for the best price that can be gotten after giving ten days publick notice and out of the money arising from the sale discharge pay and satisfy to him JOHN McCLARY his heirs the within mentioned sum of one hundred and ten pounds, two shillings with lawful Interest from the first day of November one thousand seven hundred and ninety four untill the same shall be lawfully discharged and all costs attending the drawing and recording of this Indenture and the contingent charges of the sale and all other necessary expences that shall attend the securing and obtaining the above mentioned money or performing the things that is or shall be necessary relative to the intent of this Indenture and JOHN McCLARY his heirs to pay or cause to pay the overplus if any remains from such sale to EPHRAIM SIMMONDS and MARY his Wife or their heirs; In witness whereof the said parties have hereunto set their hands and seals on the day and year within written

Sealed and delivered in presence of
PAUL his mark + McCLARY, EPHRAIM SIMMONDS
SARAH her mark + TREDWELL, JOHN McCLARY
SARAH her mark + MAYAB
At Albemarle June Court 1795
This Indenture was produced into Court and proved by the Oaths of PAUL McCLARY, SARAH TREDWELL and SARAH MAYAB, witnesses thereto, and ordered to be recorded Teste JOHN NICHOLAS C. A. C.

pp. [On margin: WELLS to WELLS, Deed]
392- KNOW ALL MEN by these presents that I MARTIN WELLS of the County of
393 Albemarle for and in consideration of forty pounds current money to me in hand paid the receipt whereof I hereby acknowledge hath and by these presents doth bargain and sell unto WILLIAM WELLS of the County of BURTON and Commonwealth of KENTUCKY one Negroe named Nan together with all future increase that may or shall hereafter arise from the Negroe, To have and to hold the bargained Negroe unto WILLIAM WELLS his heirs to his and their own proper use and I MARTIN WELLS for myself and for my heirs unto WILLIAM WELLS his heirs the bargained Negro against the right title claim or demand of any person will by these presents warrant and for ever hereafter defend, In Witness whereof I have hereunto set my hand and affixed my seal this eighteenth day of November one thousand seven hundred and ninety four
Teste JAMES FITS JARELL MARTIN WELLS
JACOB ARGEBRIGHT
WILLIAM WOOD
At Albemarle June Court 1795
This Bill of Sale was produced into Court and proved by the Oath of WILLIAM WOOD, one of the witnesses thereto, and ordered to be recorded
Teste JOHN NICHOLAS, C A C.

p. [On margin: OGG to OGG, Deed]
393 KNOW ALL MEN by these presents that I JOHN OGG of the County of Albemarle in consideration of the sum of three pounds current money of Virginia to me in hand paid by JOHN OGG, JUNIOR of the County aforesaid, the receipt whereof I do hereby acknowledge have and by these presents doth sell set over and deliver unto JOHN OGG, JUNIOR one Negroe boy named Charles, one Negroe wench named Catharine, one girl named Jemima, one Negroe girl named Delice and their increase to him JOHN OGG, JUNIOR, and I JOHN OGG for myself my heirs shall warrant and forever defend against all persons the bargained premises unto JOHN OGG, JUNIOR his heirs; In Witness whereof I have hereunto set my hand and affixed my seal this twenty eighth day of February 1795
Signed and sealed in the presence of
MICHAEL CATTERTON, JOHN his mark + OGG
THEOPHILUS KEY
MARY MERIAH HUNTSMAN
At Albemarle June County 1795
This Bill of Sale was produced into Court and proved by the Oath of MICHAEL

CATTERTON, one of the witnesses thereto, and ordered to be recorded
Teste JOHN NICHOLAS C A. C

pp. [On margin: BAILEY to HAMNER, Deed]
393- THIS INDENTURE made this first day of June in the year of our Lord one
394 thousand seven hundred and ninety five, Between WILLIAM BAILEY and
LUCY his Wife of the one part and SAMUEL HAMNER of the other part; Witnesseth that WILLIAM BAILEY and LUCY his Wife in consideration of the sum of sixty pounds current money of Virginia, the receipt whereof they do hereby acknowledge have and by these presents do bargain and sell unto SAMUEL HAMNER one certain tract of land lying in County of Albemarle on the waters of the South Fork of HARDWARE RIVER on the side of a Mountain known by the name of MITTIN MOUNTAIN and containing sixty acres be the same more or less and bounded; Begining at pointers a blazed Dogwood in said HAMNER's line runing thence South three degrees East to a Poplar on MARK LEAK's line, thence a new line runing along the side of the Mountain to a Chesnut Tree on said LEAK'S line, thence keeping said LEAK's line to pointers on SAMUEL HAMNER's line, thence keeping with HAMNER's line to pointers, thence South forty two degrees to the begining with all appurtenances, To have and to hold the tract of land with its appurtenances unto SAMUEL HAMNER his heirs and WILLIAM BAILEY and LUCY his Wife do for themselves and their heirs covenant and agree to warrant and for ever defend the land and premises from the claim of all persons; In Witness whereof they have hereunto set their hands and affixed their seals the day and year above written
WILLIAM BAILEY
LUCY BAILEY

At Albemarle June Court 1795
This Indenture was produced into Court and acknowledged by WILLIAM BAILEY, party thereto, and ordered to be recorded
Teste JOHN NICHOLAS C A C

pp. [On margin: DUKE to WEST, Deed. Examined and delivered with Commission]
394- THIS INDENTURE made this sixth day of November in the year of our Lord
395 one thousand seven hundred and ninety four; Between JAMES DUKE and
MARY his Wife of the County of HENRICO of the one part and GEORGE WEST of the County of Albemarle of the other part; Witesseth that JAMES DUKE and MARY his Wife for sundry causes but more especially for the sum of seventy five pounds lawful money of Virginia to them in hand paid by GEORGE WEST the receipt whereof they do hereby acknowledge, hath and by these presents doth bargain and sell unto GEORGE WEST his heirs one certain tract of land lying in County of Albemarle on the waters of BEAVER CREEK and bounded by the land of BERNICE BROWN, WENDEL KEABLER, JAMES GILLUM, CHRISTIAN SYLER said GEORGE WEST and JAMES BURNLEY, and courses supposed to be, Begining at a white Oak on the point of a Ridge, thence South forty four and a half degrees East one hundred and seventy two poles to a corner Stone, thence South forty eight degrees West one hundred and twenty one poles to three red Oaks near WOOD's Old Road corner to BERNICE BROWN, thence North forty four and a half degrees West one hundred and eighty poles to a white Oak, Hickory and red Oak saplings corner to

JAMES GILLUM, thence North forty one degrees East one hundred and sixty four poles to a Hickory on the side of a Hill thence South eighteen poles to a white Oak sapling on the said WEST's line, thence South seventy five degrees East twenty five poles to a white Oak on the side of a Hill, thence North fifty five degrees East twenty five and one half poles to a red Oak on the side of a Hill, thence North forty one degrees West twenty seven poles to a white Oak on the side of a Hill, thence to the first station containing by estimation two hundred acres be the same more or less with all the rents issues and profits thereof. To have and to hold the land and premises with all and singular the appurtenances unto GEORGE WEST his heirs and JAMES DUKE and MARY his Wife for themselves and their heirs will warrant and for ever defend by these presents; In Witness whereof JAMES DUKE and MARY his Wife have set their hands and seals the day and year above written Signed sealed and delivered in presence of

CHILES TERRELL, JAMES DUKE
EDMUND GOODWIN MARY DUKE
NELSON BURRUS

At Albemarle June Court 1794
This Indenture was produced into Court and acknowledged by JAMES DUKE, party thereto and ordered to be recorded
Teste JOHN CARR, Dep.Clerk

pp. [On margin: JONES to WALKER, Deed. Delivered to W. WALKER]
396- THIS INDENTURE made this thirteenth day of May in the year of our Lord
397 one thousand seven hundred and ninety five, Between LAIN JONES of Albemarle County of one part and WILLIAM WALKER of the aforesaid County of the other part; Witnesseth that LAIN JONES in consideration of sum of three hundred and seventy pounds current money to him in hand paid by WILLIAM WALKER the receipt whereof he doth hereby acknowledge, hath bargained and sold unto WILLIAM WALKER the following slaves [to wit] Nat, James, Peggy, Silla, Lucy, Sall, Joice and Fanny together with the future increase of the female slaves, To have and to hold the eight slaves and their future increase to WILLIAM WALKER his heirs and LAIN JONES doth bind himself his heirs to warrant and defend the right and title of the eight slaves with their future increase against the claim of any person, Provided nevertheless if LAIN JONES his heirs do pay or cause to be paid unto WILLIAM WALKER his heirs one hundred and twenty three pounds, six shillings and eight pence current money the 25th day of December one thousand seven hundred and ninety six and one hundred and twenty three pounds, six shillings and eight pence like money the 25th day of December one thousand seven hundred and ninety seven and one hundred and twenty three pound, six shillings and eight pence like money the 25th day of December one thousand seven hundred and ninety eight, and for which LAIN JONES has executed this day to WILLIAM WALKER three Bonds for one hundred twenty three pounds, six shillings and eight pence current money payable at the times specifyed in this Indenture as this Mortgage is taken as security for the payment of the sums of money; Now if LAIN JONES his heirs do pay or cause to be paid to WILLIAM WALKER his heirs the aforesaid recited sums of money at the time specified then this Mortgage to be void or else to remain in full force and virtue; In Witness whereof LAIN JONES hath hereunto set his hand and affixed his seal

the day and year afore written
Signed sealed and acknowledged in presence of
MARTIN DAVENPORT, LAIN JONES
NICHOLAS [[
JOHN JONES
At Albemarle June Court 1795
This Indenture was produced into Court and acknowledged by LAIN JONES, party thereto, and ordered to be recorded
Teste JOHN NICHOLAS C A C

p. [On margin: CRENSHAW to FLANAGAN, Release]
397 KNOW ALL MEN by these presents that I DAVID CRENSHAW of LOUISA County have and by these presents do release quit claim and confirm unto JAMES FLANNAGAN all the right title and interest which I have in two hundred and thirty three acres of land lying in the County of Albemarle being part of a tract of land mortgaged to me by JAMES FLANNAGAN now in his possession by virtue of a Deed made to him by WILLIAM CRENSHAW for Debt due me and DAVID CRENSHAW doth release the right title and interest to JAMES FLANNAGAN and his heirs, In Witness whereof I have subscribed my name and affixed my seal this eighteenth day of November one thousand seven hundred and ninety four
Signed sealed and delivered in presence of
THOMAS FRETWELL DAVID CRENSHAW
DRURY WOOD
JAMES LINDSAY
DAVID WOOD
At Albemarle June Court 1795
This Deed of Release was produced into Court and proved by the Oaths of THOMAS FRETWELL, DRURY WOOD and JAMES LINDSAY, three of the witnesses thereto and ordered to be recorded
Teste JOHN CARR, Dep Clerk

pp. [On margin: DOWELL to DOWELL, Deed]
397- THIS INDENTURE made the twenty second day of April one thousand seven
399 seven hundred and ninety five; Between WILLIAM DOWELL of the County of Albemarle of one part and his Son, RICHARD DOWELL, of the other part; Witnesseth that WILLIAM DOWELL in consideration of the uses and trusts hereafter mentioned and for the consideration of five shillings to him in hand paid, the receipt whereof he doth hereby acknowledge, hath and by these presents doth bargain sell and release unto RICHARD DOWELL his heirs in Trust for the uses hereafter mentioned the tract of land whereon WILLIAM DOWELL now lives lying in County of Albemarle and containing one hundred acres be the same more or less the said WILLIAM DOWELL for the use and trust hereafter mentioned and for the consideration hath also given and delivered by thse presents unto RICHARD DOWELL his heirs in Trust for the uses hereafter mentioned three head of Cattle marked with a swallow fork in the left ear and underkeel in the right ear, one Roan Colt three years old this Spring, five head of sheep with the mark as the Cattle, two feather beds bedstead and furniture, one desk, one cubbard, one black Walnut table, cotton and flax

wheel, seven chairs, one pewter dish, three basons and seven plates with all the earthen ware and other household stuff belonging to WILLIAM DOWELL; To have and to hold the lands goods and chattels together with all and singular the improvements thereon and appurtenances thereunto belonging unto RICHARD DOWELL his heirs on the following terms and conditions, that is to say, that whereas WILLIAM DOWELL is justly indebted to ROBERT and ARCHIBALD WILSON of the County of ORANGE the full and just sum of twenty seven pounds, seventeen shillings and three pence half penny of the present current money of Virginia by Bond bearing date the twentieth instant and in case WILLIAM DOWELL shall well and truly pay ROBERT and ARCHIBALD WILSON the aforesaid sum with legal Interest from the fourteenth day of August last on or before the first day of December next ensuing that in that case the right and title of the aforesaid land, goods and chattels shall be again vested in WILLIAM DOWELL but if he fails for to pay the Debt by the time aforesaid that RICHARD DOWELL shall expose the land goods and chattels to sale to the highest bidder for ready money and out of the money arising by such sale pay to ROBERT and ARCHIBALD WILSON the aforesaid debt and Interest and after deducting the expences and charges attending such sale together with the expences of recording this Deed return the residue if any unto WILLIAM DOWELL who hereby obliges himself and his heirs to warrant and defend the right and title of the land goods and chattels to any purchaser, In Testimony whereof the parties hath hereunto set their hands and affixed their seals the day and year first above written
Signed sealed and delivered in presence of

DAVID GILLASPY, WILLIAM his mark X DOWELL
BASSELL his mark X GLASS RICHARD DOWELL
JOHN his mark X WARNSLEY

At Albemarle June Court 1795
This Indenture was produced into Court and proved by the Oaths of DAVID GILLASPY, BASSELL GLASS and JOHN WARNSLEY, witnesses thereto, and ordered to be recorded Teste JOHN NICHOLAS, C A C.

p. [On margin: FORTUNE to BOLES, Deed]
399 THIS INDENTURE made this twenty eighth day of January one thousand seven hundred and ninety five; Between WILLIAM FORTUNE of Albemarle County of one part and NATHAN BOWLES of the said County of the other part; Witnesseth that WILLIAM FORTUNE in consideration of the sum of forty pounds current money to him in hand paid the receipt whereof he doth hereby acknowledge hath bargained and sold unto NATHAN BOWLES a certain tract of land lying in County of Albemarle on the South side of BEAVERDAM CREEK containing forty acres be the same more or less adjoining the lands of said NATHAN BOWLES, JOHN COLES, MARTIN DAVENPORT and said WILLIAM FORTUNE, together with all appurtenances thereunto belonging; To have and to hold the land with the appurtenances to NATHAN BOWLES his heirs and WILLIAM FORTUNE his heirs will warrant the right and title to the tract of land by these presents against the claim of any person to NATHAN BOWLES his heirs; In Witness whereof WILLIAM FORTUNE hath hereunto set his hand and seal the day and date above written
Signed sealed and delivered in presence of

SAMUEL DYER, WILLIAM his mark X FORTUNE

WILLIAM MOORE
REUBIN COBBS
JOHN CLARKSON

At Albemarle June Court 1795
This Indenture was produced into Court and acknowledged by WILLIAM FORTUNE party thereto, and ordered to be recorded
Teste JOHN NICHOLAS C A C

p. [On margin: FORTUNE to BOLES, Deed]
400 THIS INDENTURE made the first day of June in the year of our Lord one thousand seven hundred and ninety five; Between WILLIAMSON FORTUNE of Albemarle County of one part and NATHAN BOWLES of the aforesaid County of the other part; Witnesseth that WILLIAMSON FORTUNE in consideration of the sum of seventy five pounds current money of Virginia to him in hand paid by NATHAN BOWLES, the receipt whereof he doth hereby acknowledge, hath and by these presents doth bargain and sell unto NATHAN BOWLES his heirs a certain tract of land lying in County of Albemarle containing by estimation one hundred and eight acres be the same more or less and bounded; Begining at pointers corner to STRINGER in JOHN COLES's line, thence along COLES's line North thirty five degrees East twenty poles to a white Oak, thence North ten degrees East fifty poles to a white Oak, thence North five degrees West twenty poles to pointers, South eighty degrees West twenty one poles to pointers, North sixty five degrees West thirty six poles to pointers, North sixty four degrees West seventy four poles to a Pine standing on the GREEN MOUNTAIN ROAD, thence along the GREEN MOUNTAIN ROAD to where it intersects another Road, then down that and same marked lines varying a little from the Road thirty one poles to the begining, To have and to hold the land and premises with all the appurtenances thereunto belonging unto NATHAN BOWLES his heirs and WILLIAMSON FORTUNE his heirs doth hereby covenant with NATHAN BOWLES his heirs the tract of land and premises with all appurtenances against the claim of all persons will warrant and forever defend by these presents, In Witness whereof WILLIAMSON FORTUNE hath hereunto set his hand and affixed his seal the day and year above written

Signed sealed and delivered in presence of

ISAAC MILLER, WILLIAMSON FORTUNE
JAMES his mark X BAILEY
JOHN BARRET

At Albemarle June Court 1795
This Indenture was produced into Court and acknowledged by WILLIAMSON FORTUNE, party thereto, and ordered to be recorded
Teste JOHN NICHOLAS, C. A. C.

p. [On margin: BALLEW to RODERICK Delivered F. RODERICK this 12th of
401 February 1813]

THIS INDENTURE made this first day of June in the year of our Lord one thousand seven hundred and ninety five; Between PETER BELEW of County of Albemarle of the one part and FREDERICK RODERICK of the same County of the other part; Witnesseth that PETER BELEW for and in consideration of the sum of

six pounds current money of Virginia to him in hand paid by FREDERICK RODERICK the receipt whereof he doth hereby acknowledge, hath and by these presents doth bargain and sell unto FREDERICK RODERICK and to his heirs, a certain tract of land lying in County of Albemarle on the waters of MECHUMS RIVER containing eight acres, Begining at a Pine on JAMES COLLEY's and JOHN BENT's line runing thence South forty seven degrees West fifty four poles to a Pine in JAMES COLLEY's line, thence with new lines South eleven degrees East twenty four poles to a Pine and Oak sapling in WADE VYER's line, North forty seven degrees East thirty four poles to several saplins in JOHN BENT's line, North eleven degrees West twenty four poles to the begining; together with all appurtenances thereunto belonging; To have and to hold the tract of land with appurtenances unto FREDERICK RODERICK his heirs and PETER BELEW for himself and his heirs doth covenant with FREDERICK RODERICK his heirs against the claim of all persons shall warrant and for ever defend by these presents; In Witness whereof PETER BELEW hath hereunto set his hand and affixed his seal the day and year above written
Sealed and delivered in presence of

RICHARD H. ALLEN, PETER his mark X BELEW
ALEXANDER WATSON
THOMAS BELL

At Albemarle June Court 1795
This Indenture was presented into Court and acknowledged by PETER BELEW party thereto and ordered to be recorded
Teste JOHN NICHOLAS C. A. C.

pp. [On margin: MULLINS's Exrs. to EWELL, Deed]
402- THIS INDENTURE made this twentieth day of February one thousand seven
403 hundred and ninety five; Between CONERLY MULLINS and JAMES ALLEN, Executors of JOHN MULLINS, deceased, and HENRY MULLINS Heir at Law of GOOCHLAND County on the one part and MAXARY EWELL of Albemarle County on the other part; Witnesseth that CONERLY MULLINS, JAMES ALLEN and HENRY MULLINS in consdieration of the sum of one hundred and ten pounds current money to them in hand paid by MAXARY EWELL, the receipt whereof they do hereby acknowledge, hath and by these presents doth bargain and sell unto MAXARY EWELL his heirs a certain tract of land containing three hundred and eight acres be the same more or less, lyinjg in the County of Albemarle which land is granted to us CONERLY MULLINS, JAMES ALLEN by Patent and being bounded; lying on both sides of DOYLE's RIVER and joining JOHN MULLINS, JOHN MAUPIN, WILLIAM JARMAN and THOMAS JARMAN, To have and to hold the land and premises with all and singular the appurtenances thereunto belonging to MAXARY EWELL his heirs as if the same were granted to him by Patent and CONERLY MULLINS and JAMES ALLEN do hereby bind themseles their heirs to warrant and forever defend the land unto MAXARY EWELL his heirs, In Witness whereof CONERLY MULLINS, JAMES ALLEN and HENRY MULLINS, Heir at Law, hath set their hands and seals the day and year above written
Signed sealed and delivered in the presence of

THOMAS J. PRICE as to all CONERLY MULLINS
ELIZABETH her mark X EWELL JAMES ALLEN

THOMAS EWELL as to CM & HM HENRY MULLINS
JOHN MULLINS, JUNR.
BEZALEEL BROWN as to James Allen

Memorandum: That on this twentieth day of February 1795 full and peaceable possession and seizen was given and granted by CONERLY MULLINS, JAMES ALLEN and HENRY MULLINS of the within mentioned land with the appurtenances unto MAXARY EWELL his heirs according to the true intent purport and meaning of the present Indenture in the presence of us

JOHN MULLINS, SENR. CONERLY MULLINS
THOMAS J. PRICE HENRY MULLINS
ELIZABETH her mark X EWELL
THOMAS EWELL,
JOHN MULLINS, JUNR.

Then received of MAXARY EWELL full satisfaction for the within Deed this day and date above mentioned, Witness our hands and seals
Signed in the presence of us

JOHN MULLINS, SENR. CONERLY MULLINS
THOMAS J. PRICE HENRY MULLINS
ELIZABETH her mark X EWELL,
THOMAS EWELL
JOHN MULLINS, JUNR.

At Albemarle June Court 1795
This Indenturre was produced into Court and proved by the Oaths of JOHN MULLINS, SENR and THOMAS JOHNSON PRICE as to CONERLY MULLINS, JAMES ALLEN and HENRY MULLINS; by the Oath of THOMAS EWELL as to CONERLY MULLINS and HENRY MULLINS, and by the Oath of BEZALEEL BROWN as to JAMES ALLEN, the witnesses thereto, and ordered to be recorded
Teste JOHN NICHOLAS, C. A. C.

pp. [On margin: KERR to DIVERS, Deed]
404- THIS INDENTURE made this first day of June in the year of our Lord one
405 thousand seven hundred and ninety five; Between JAMES KERR of the County of Albemarle of one part and GEORGE DIVERS of the same County of the other part; Witnesseth that JAMES KERR in consideratiion of the sum of eighty seven pounds, five shillings current money of Virginia in hand paid, the receipt whereof he doth acknowledge, hath bargained and sold unto GEORGE DIVERS and to his heirs one certain tract of land situate on the North side of the Road leading from CHARLOTTESVILLE to STAUNTON in the County of Albemarle and is bounded; Begining at a corner Hickory on the Road, thence down the same agreeable to the courses thereof one hundred and five and one quarter poles to pointers on the Road, thence North three degrees West one hundred and seven poles to a corner Maple, North seventy one degrees West one hundred and fifteen poles to pointers on said DIVERS's line, thence South six and three quarters degrees East one hundred and sixty three poles to the begining, containing eighty seven and one quarter acres; To have and to hold the eighty seven and one quarter acres of land to GEORGE DIVERS his heirs together with all appurtenances thereunto belonging, and JAMES KERR for himself and his heirs doth covenant and agree with GEORGE DIVERS his heirs shall

shall for ever hold and enjoy the tract of land; In Witness whereof JAMES KERR hath hereunto set his hand and affixed his seal the day and year first above written Signed sealed and delivered in the presence of

[no witnesses recorded] JAMES KERR

Memorandum: That on the day and date of the within written Deed quiet and peaceable possesson and seizin of the land and premises within mentioned was had and taken by the within mentioned JAMES KERR and by him delivered to the within named GEORGE DIVERS according to the tenor form and effect of the within Deed

JAMES KERR

June 1st 1795. Received of GEORGE DIVERS eighty seven pounds, five shillings current money it being the consideration money within mentioned

JAMES KERR

At Albemarle June Court 1795
This Indenture was produced into Court and acknowledged by JAMES KERR, party thereto, and ordered to be recorded

Teste JOHN NICHOLAS, C. A. C.

pp. [On margin: CARTER to SCHENK & LOTT, Deed of Trust]
405- THIS INDENTURE made this sixth day of March in the year of our Lord one
406 thousand seven hundred and ninety five; Between HENRY CARTER of the County of Albemarle of the first part; CORNELIUS SCHENK and PETER LOTT of the same County of the second part and ROBERT and WILLIAM WARDLOW of the third part; Witnesseth that HENRY CARTER in consideration of the sum of twenty one pounds, three shillings and three pence to him in hand paid which HENRY CARTER doth acknowledge to be justly due to CORNLIUS SCHENK and PETER LOTT and honestly desires to secure and pay to them and also in consideration of the sum of five shillings to him in hand paid by ROBERT and WILLIAM WARDLOW the receipt whereof he doth hereby acknowledge hath and by these presents doth bargain and sell unto ROBERT and WILLIAM WARDLOW and their heirs a tract of land in the County of Albemarle and containing thirty five acres, BLAND BALLARD on the East. ROWLAND HORSLEY on the South, THOMAS BURTON on the West and MRS. SHIFLET on the North with the improvements thereon, one gray mare four years old branded P B on the near buttock, two cows six years old, two yearlings red and black each, seven head of hogs and three ewes and one lamb; To have and to hold the property to them ROBERT and WILLIAM WARDLOW their heirs, yet upon this special Trust that ROBERT and WILLIAM WARDLOW shall on or before the sixth day of March one thousand seven hundred and ninety six, if thereunto required by CORNELIUS SCHENK and PETER LOTT their heirs dispose of the aforesaid property to the best bidder and having sold shall convey and deliver the property to the purchasers and pay the money to CORNELIUS SCHENK and PETER LOTT their heirs or as much thereof as will satisfy the aforesaid debt with lawful Interest together with the expence of writing and recording this Indenture and the contingent charges attending the sale and the remainder returned if there should be any to HENRY CARTER his heirs, Nevertheless provided always if HENRY CARTER shall before the sixth day of March one thousand seven hundred and ninety six pay CORNELIUS SCHENK and PETER LOTT the sum of twenty one pounds, three shillings and three pence with legal

Interest then ROBERT and WILLIAM WARDLOW will reconvey the aforementioned property to HENRY CARTER his heirs and HENRY CARTER doth agree with ROBERT and WILLIAM WARDLOW their heirs that the property to ROBERT and WILLIAM WARDLOW their heirs &c. against the claim of all persons will warrant and for ever defend, In Witness whereof HENRY CARTER hath hereunto set his hand and seal the day and year above written

Signed sealed and delivered in presence of

JOHN JOUETT, HENRY CARTER
T. W. LEWIS,
JOHN T. GILMER

At Albemarle June Court 1795

This Indenture was produced into Court and proved by the Oaths of JOHN JOUETT, THOMAS W. LEWIS and JOHN T. GILMER, witnesses thereto, and ordered to be recorded Teste JOHN NICHOLAS, C A C

p. [On margin: MELTON's Trustees to USHER, Deed]
407 THIS INDENTURE made this fourteenth day of July in the year of our Lord one thousand seven hundred and ninety four; Between CHARLES L. LEWIS, WILLIAM CLARK, HOWELL LEWIS and EDWARD MOORE, a majority of the Trustees for the Town of MELTON by an Act of Assembly of the one part and JAMES USHER of County of Albemarle of other part; Witnesseth that CHARLES L. LEWIS, WILLIAM CLARK, HOWELL LEWIS and EDWARD MOORE by virtue of an Act of Assembly for establishing the Town of MELTON on the lands of BENNET HENDERSON in the County of Albemarle and in consideration of the sum of fifteen pounds current money of Virginia to them in hand paid by JAMES USHER, the receipt whereof they do hereby acknowledge, hath bargained and sold unto JAMES USHER and to his heirs a certain lott or parcel of ground containing half an acre and marked in the Plan of the Town number [34], To have and to hold the lott of ground with all appurtenances unto JAMES USHER and to his heirs and CHARLES L. LEWIS, WILLIAM CLARK, HOWELL LEWIS and EDWARD MOORE doth covenant and agree that the parcel of ground with appurtenances thereunto belonging with JAMES USHER and his heirs that they will warrant and for ever defend against the claim of all persons; In Witness whereof the parties aforesaid hath hereunto set their hands and affixed their seals the day and year first above written

Signed sealed and delivered in the presence of

JOHN THOMAS CHARLES L. LEWIS
BENNET HENDERSON WILLIAM CLARK
W. D. MERIWETHER HOWELL LEWIS
EDWARD MOORE

At Albemarle October Court 1794

This Indenture was produced into Court and proved by the Oaths of BENNET HENDERSON and WILLIAM D. MERIWETHER, two of the witnesses thereto, And at June Court 1795, was further proved by the Oath of JOHN THOMAS, a third witness thereto and ordered to be recorded

Teste JOHN NICHOLAS, C. A. C.

pp. [On margin: MAUPIN to BROWN, Deed]
408- THIS INDENTURE made this nineteenth day of December one thousand
409 seven hundred and ninety four; Between ZACHARIAS MAUPIN of one part of Albemarle and JOHN BROWN of said County of other part; Witnesseth that ZACHARIAS MAUPIN in consideration of the sum of thirty eight pounds current money of Virginia to him in hand paid by JOHN BROWN the receipt whereof he doth hereby acknowledge, hath and by these presents doth bargain and sell unto JOHN BROWN and to his heirs one certain tract of land containing eighty seven acres and a quarter lying in County of Albemarle on the North side of BEAVER CREEK on the MEETING HOUSE ROAD bounded, Begining at pointers runing South thirty eight degrees East fifty poles to a corner in said BROWN's line, North eighty degrees West one hundred and forty poles to a corner Poplar near a Branch, North fifty degrees West nineteen poles to a Pine on the same Branch, North twenty five degrees West forty eight poles to a white Oak on the said Branch, North forty degrees West twenty one poles to a Spanish Oak, North eleven degrees West thirty eight poles to a Maple on a Branch near the Old Road, North six degrees West forty poles to a corner Pine, North seventy three degrees West seventy nine poles crossing the MEETING HOUSE ROAD to BROWN's line, thence along BROWN's line to the begining South fourteen degrees East seventeen poles to pointers , South thirty three degrees East one hundred and seventeen poles to pointers at the begining; To have and to hold the tract of land with appurtenances unto JOHN BROWN and his heirs and ZACHARIAS MAUPIN for himself and his heirs will warrant and forever defend the land and premises against all persons laying any claim thereunto; In Witness whereof JOHN BROWN hath hereunto set his hand and affixed his seal this 19th day of December one thousand seven hundred and ninety four

Signed sealed and delivered in presence of

ALLEN HILL ZACHARIAS MAUPIN
HENRY SAILER
WENDLE KEABLER

Memorandum: That on the 19th day of December one thousand seven hundred and ninety four ZACHARIAS MAUPIN gave JOHN BROWN peaceable possession and seizin of the land and tenements within menioned which was delivered by ZACHARIAS MAUPIN to JOHN BROWN according to the form and effect of the within written Deed

Teste In presence of

ALLEN HILL, ZACHARIAS MAUPIN
HENRY SAILER,
WENDLE KEABLER

Received of the within named JOHN BROWN the sum of thirty eight pounds current money of Virginia which is the consideration money in the Deed mentioned

Teste ALLEN HILL, ZACHARIAS MAUPIN
HENRY SAILER
WINDLE KEABLER

At Albemarle April Court 1795

This Indenture was produced into Court and proved by the Oaths of HENRY SAILER and WENDLE KEABLER two of the witnesses thereto, And at June Court 1795, was further proved by the Oath of ZACHARIAS MAUPIN, party thereto and ordered to be recorded

Teste JOHN NICHOLAS, C. A. C.

p. [On margin: CLARKE to JORDAN, Deed]
410 THIS INDENTURE made this first day of June in the year of our Lord one thousand seven hundred and ninety five; Between WILLIAM CLARK for the Commonwealth of Virginia of the one part and BENJAMIN JORDAN of the other part; Witnesseth that WILLIAM CLARK in consideration of the sum of five shillings to him in hand paid for the use of the Commonwealth of Virginia the receipt whereof he doth hereby acknowledge, hath on behalf of the Commonwealth of Virginia pursuant to an Act of the General Assembly authorizing WILLIAM CLARK to sell and convey sundry tracts of land agreeable to a Clause in the Revenue Act to satisfy the taxes due thereon have bargained and sold unto BENJAMIN JORDAN his heirs a certain tract of land containing eighteen acres lying in Albemarle County and being part of a larger tract enrolled in the name of THOMAS COLDER and bounded, Begining at a corner on a Branch and runing thence South twenty one degrees West twenty eight poles to pointers, South five degrees East one hundred poles, North seventy five degrees West one hundred and seven poles to the begining; To have and to hold the land and premises with the appurtenances unto BENJAMIN JORDAN and his heirs, In Witness whereof WILLIAM CLARK on behalf of the Commonwealth of Virginia hath set his hand and affixed his seal the day and year first above written

Signed sealed and delivered in the presence of

[no witnesses recorded] WILLIAM CLARK

At Albemarle June Court 1795

This Indenture was produced into Court and acknowledged by WILLIAM CLARK, party thereto, and ordered to be recorded

Teste JOHN NICHOLAS C. A. C.

p. [On margin: GOOCH to DOVE, Deed]
411 THIS INDENTURE made the first day of June in the year of our Lord one thousand seven hundred and ninety five; Between WILLIAM GOOCH and LUCY his Wife of the County of Albemarle of one part and THOMAS DOVE of the same County of the other part; Witnesseth that WILLIAM GOOCH in consideration of the sum of twenty pounds current money of Virginia to him in hand paid hath bargained and sold unto THOMAS DOVE and his heirs a tract of land containing by estimation fifty five acres be the same more or less and bounded; Begining on PHILIP GOOCH's line and runing thence to SAMUEL DEDMAN's line, To have and to hold the tract of land with the appurtenances unto THOMAS DOVE and his heirs and WILLIAM GOOCH his heirs will warrant and for ever defend the tract of land and premises with all appurtenances unto THOMAS DOVE and his heirs against the claim of all persons; In Witness whereof WILLIAM GOOCH hath hereunto set his hand and affixed his seal the day and year above written

Signed sealed and delivered in presence of

[no witnesses recorded] WILLIAM GOOCH

At Albemarle June Court 1795

This Indenture was produced into Court and acknowledged by WILLIAM GOOCH,

party thereto and ordered to be recorded
Teste JOHN NICHOLAS, C. A. C.

pp. [On margin: HARRISON to BALLARD, Deed]
411- THIS INDENTURE made this fourth day of April one thousand seven hundred
412 and ninety four; Between JAMES HARRISON and SARAH his Wife of one part and JOHNSON BALLARD of the other part; Witnesseth that JAMES HARRISON and SARAH his Wife in consideration of the sum of twenty five pounds current money of Virginia to them in hand paid by JOHNSON BALLARD the receipt whereof they do hereby acknowledge, hath and by these presents doth bargain and sell unto JOHNSON BALLARD and his heirs a certain tract of land situate in County of Albemarle and on the East side of JAMES KEATON's Spring Branch and bounded, Begining on JAMES KEATON's line when it crosses said KEATON's Spring Branch thence down the Branch to WILLIAM VIA's line, thence along VIA's line to JAMES HARRISON's corner at the foot of JONES's MOUNTAIN, thence on HARRISON's line to JAMES KEATON's corner, thence along KEATON's and HARRISON's line to the begining estimated at fifty acres more or less, To have and to hold the tract of land with appurtenances unto JOHNSON BALLARD his heirs and JAMES HARRISON and SARAH his Wife do covenant with JOHNSON BALLARD his heirs that the parcel of land with its appurtenances he will warrant and for ever defend against the claim of any person; In Witness whereof JAMES HARRISON and SARAH his Wife have hereunto set their hands and seals the day and year above written

Signed sealed and delivered in presence of

BAZELEEL BROWN,	JAMES HARRISON
THOMAS HARRIS,	SARAH HARRISON
NATHAN HARRIS	
CORNELIUS MAUPIN	

1794. Then received of JOHNSON BALLARD the sum of twenty five pounds current money of Virginia it being in full for the consideration mentioned in the within Deed

JAMES HARRISON

At Albemarle June Court 1795
This Indenture was produced into Court and proved by the Oaths of BAZELEEL BROWN, NATHAN HARRIS and CORNELIUS MAUPIN, three of the witnesses thereto, and ordered to be recorded
Teste JOHN NICHOLAS C. A. C.

pp. [On margin: BALLARD to BROWN, Deed]
412- THIS INDENTURE made this tenth day of March in the year of our Lord one
413 thousand seven hundred and ninety five, Between JOHNSON BALLARD, JAMES HARRISON and SARAH his Wife of the County of Albemarle of the one part and BAZELEEL BROWN of the same County of the other part; Witnesseth that JOHNSON BALLARD, JAMES HARRISON and SARAH his Wife in consideration of the sum of one hundred Dollars current money of Virginia the receipt whereof JOHNSON BALLARD, JAMES HARRISON and SARAH his Wife doth acknowledge, hath and by these presents doth bargain and sell unto BAZELEEL

BROWN his heirs one certain tract of land containing one hundred acres situate in County of Albemarle and on the North side of DOYLES RIVER adjoining the lands of BENAJAH BROWN, WILLIAM BRUCE, DAVID CRAIG and the said BAZELEEL BROWN, and bounded, Begining at a small Field cornering on BAZELEEL BROWN in BENAJAH BROWN's line, thence along BENAJAH BROWN's, WILLIAM BRUCE's and DAVID CRAIG's lines South twenty two degrees East two hundred and eighty nine poles to a Branch cornering on a dead Oak, thence down the Branch South six degrees West twelve poles to a bent on the Branch, thence meandering with the Branch South seventeen degrees West twenty poles to a white Oak, thence South thirty one degrees West thirty three poles to pointers, thence North seventy two degrees West two hundred and fifty poles to pointers in BEZALEEL BROWN's line, thence North and on said BROWN's line seventy two poles to the begining; To have and to hold the tract of land with all and singular the premises with all appurtenances thereunto belonging unto BAZELEEL BROWN his heirs and JOHNSON BALLARD, JAMES HARRISON and SARAH his Wife and their heirs the tract of land with its appurtenances unto BAZELEEL BROWN his heirs will warrant and defend by these presents; In Witness whereof JOHNSON BALLARD, JAMES HARRISON and SARAH his Wife have hereunto set their hands and seals the day and year above written

Signed sealed and delivered in presence of

MAXARY EWELL, JOHNSON his mark X BALLARD
THOMAS HARRIS, JAMES HARRISON
THOMAS J. PRICE SARAH HARRISON
BENAJAH BROWN

At Albemarle June Court 1795

This Indenture was produced into Court and proved by the Oaths of MAXARY EWELL, THOMAS HARRIS and THOMAS J. PRICE, three of the witnesses thereto, and ordered to be recorded

Teste JOHN CARR, Dep. Clerk

p. [On margin: MAUPIN to MAUPIN Deed]
414 THIS INDENTURE made this first day of June in the year of our Lord one thousand seven hundred and ninety five, Between DANUEL MAUPIN G.S. of Albemarle County of the one part and MATTHEW MAUPIN, G. S., of the same County of the other part; Witnesseth that DANIEL MAUPIN in consideration of the sum of forty five pounds current money of Virginia to him in hand paid the receipt whereof he doth acknowledge, hath and by these presents doth bargain and sell unto MATTHEW MAUPIN his heirs one certain tract of land lying in County of Albemarle on the YELLOW BRANCH adjoining of WILLIAM MAUPIN, SENR. on the North side and BLAND MAUPIN on the West bounded; Begining at a white Oak on the YELLOW BRANCH from thence up the Branch to a Maple thence across a Chesnut Oak adjoining CORNELIUS MAUPIN on the South side, thence to a Dogwood on the same side adjoining JOHN MAUPIN, To have and to hold the tract of land and premises with all and singular the appurtenances thereunto belonging unto MATTHEW MAUPIN his heirs and DANIEL MAUPIN his heirs doth hereby covenant with MATTHEW MAUPIN his heirs the land and premises with appurtenances will warrant and forever defend free from the claim of any person; In Witness where-

of DANIEL MAUPIN hath hereunto set his hand and seal the day and year above written

DANIEL MAUPIN
JEAN MAUPIN

At Albemarle June Court 1795
This Indenture was produced into Court and acknowledged by DANIEL MAUPIN and JEAN his Wife, she being first privily examined as the Law directs, and ordered to be recorded Teste JOHN NICHOLAS, C.A. C.

p. [On margin: CARR's Executors to CARR, Deed]
415 THIS INDENTURE made and done this fifteenth day of February one thousand seven hundred and ninety four, Between THOMAS CARR and McCAGER CARR, Executors of GIDEON CARR, deceased, both of the County of Albemarle of the one part and JOHN CARR of the County aforesaid of the other part; [Witnesseth] that THOMAS CARR and McCAGER CARR, Executors of GIDEON CARR, deceased, for sundry good causes but more especially in consideratiion of the sum of one hundred and seventy five pounds current money of Virginia to them in hand paid the receipt whereof they do acknowledge, hath and by these presents doth bargain and sell unto JOHN CARR his heirs all that tract of land lying in County of Albemarle and bounded; Begining at a Chesnut Stump, thence North eighty eight degrees West one hundred eighty three poles to a white Oak bush in JOHN KEY's line and DAVID WOOD's corner, thence South fifty seven degrees East one hundred and ninety poles to pointers in DAVID WOOD's line, thence North thirty eight and a half degrees East one hundred and forty six poles to a Hickory in McCAGER CARR's line, from thence along his line to the first station containing by estimation three hundred acres be the same more or less, together with all houses orchards rents issues and profits thereof; To have and to hold the tract of land hereby granted unto JOHN CARR his heirs and THOMAS CARR and McCAGER CARR, Executors as aforesaid, will warrant and forever defend by these presents; In Witness wherof the parties to these presents have fixt their hands and seals the day and year above written
Signed sealed and delivered in the presence of

[no witnesses recorded] THOMAS CARR
MICAJAH CARR

Received of JOHN CARR the full and just sum of one hundred and seventy five pounds current money of Virginia in full satisfaction according to the form and effect of the within Deed this day and year within written

THOMAS CARR
MICAJAH CARR

At Albemarle June Court 1795
This Indenture was produced into Court and acknowledged by THOMAS CARR and MICAJAH CARR, parties thereto, and ordered to be recorded
Teste JOHN NICHOLAS, C. A. C.

p. [On margin: CLUSMAN to SCHENK & LOTT, Deed]
416 THIS INDENTURE made this fourth day of December in the year of our Lord one thousand seven hundred and ninety four; Between HANNAH CLUSMAN of the County of Albemarle and Town of CHARLOTTESVILLE of one part and

CORNELIUS SCHENK and PETER LOTT of County of Albemarle and same Town of the other part; Witnesseth that HANNAH CLUSMAN hath bargained and sold unto CORNELIUS SCHENK and PETER LOTT a Negro girl named Alce and a house and lot distinguished in the plan of the Town by the number [71 [seventy one, To have and to hold the Negro with her increase and the house and lott with all its appurtenances and improvements to their proper use, provided always and these presents are upon this condition that if HANNAH CLUSMAN shall pay or cause to be paid to CORNELIUS SCHENK and PETER LOTT the just sum of thirty six pounds lawfull money of Virginia on or before the fourth day of December one thousand seven hundred and ninety five with lawfull Interest from the date hereof and the expence of recording this Writing, then this Obligation to be void or else remain in force and further that the property is not under any incumbrance and the said HANNAH doth hereby warrant and defend the same against the claim of all persons to CORNELIUS SCHENK and PETER LOTT their heirs; In Witnss whereof HANNAH CLUSMAN hath hereunto set her hand and affixed her seal the day and year above written

Signed sealed and delivered in presence of

F. TALIAFERRO, HANNAH her mark X CLUSMAN
JOSEPH KENNEDY
GEORGE BRUCE

At Albemarle December Court 1794

This Indenture was produced into Court and acknowledged by HANNAH CLUSMAN party thereto and ordered to be recorded

Teste JOHN NICHOLAS C. A. C.

pp. [On margin: DANDRIDGE to WEBB, Release]
416- TO ALL TO WHOM these presents shall come, I WILLIAM DANDRIDGE
417 of County of NEW KENT, send Greeting; Whereas LEWIS WEBB of the County of NEW KENT was on the first day of August in the year of our Lord 1788 indebted to WILLIAM DANDRIDGE by his certain Bill Penal in the sum of forty six pounds, seven shillings and seven pence three farthings and on the 1st day of August did also grant his Note to FRANCIS BAKER for the further sum of fourteen pounds, ten shillings payable on the 25th day of December then next ensuing which Note was afterwards assigned by FRANCIS BAKER to WILLIAM DANDRIDGE and whereas afterwards LEWIS WEBB being seized and possessed in his demesne as of fee of and in a certain tract of land situate in County of Albemarle called and known by the name of WEBB's MOUNTAIN and being willing and desirous of securing the payment of the said several sums of money together with the Interest respectively occuring thereon did on the sixth day of April in the year of our Lord 1789, by his certain Deed of Mortgage, convey to WILLIAM DANDRIDGE his heirs all the said tract of land upon the proviso that if LEWIS WEBB should well and truly pay or cause to be paid unto WILLIAM DANDRIDGE the several sums of money together with the legal Interest thereon accruing from the time they became due when he should be thereto required that then and in such case the Deed of Mortgage should become null and void and whereas LEWIS WEBB and certain of his Creditors having right to claim payment out of the sale of the land have authorized Mr. DAVID BULLOCK of the County of LOUISA, Attorney at Law, to dispose of the land to the best advan-

tage, Now Know ye that WILLIAM DANDRIDGE in consideration of the sum of forty six pounds, seven shillings and seven pence three farthings together with Interest from the first day of August 1788 and the additional sum of fourteen pounds, ten shillngs together with the Interest from the twenty fifth day of December 1789, being first duly paid and satisfied to Mr. DAVID BULLOCK for my use do hereby for myself and my heirs do freely and absolutely release and for ever quit claim of in or to the mortgaged premises and the appurtenances and to all the Estate and title which I the said WILLIAM DANDRIDGE or any one claiming by through or under me might otherwise claim therein. In Witness whereof I have hereunto set my hand and affixed my seal this 30th day of December 1792

Sealed and delivered in the presence of

BENJAMIN STRANGE WILLIAM DANDRIDGE
F. BAKER
THOMAS ELLIOTT

At a Court held for NEW KENT County the 10th of October 1793.
This Deed of Release was acknowledged by WILLIAM DANDRIDGE, party thereto, and ordered to be recorded

Teste WILLIAM CLAYTON C. O C.

At Albemarle July Court 1795
This Release was produced into Court and being certifyed by WILLIAM CLAYTON, Clerk of NEW KENT County, as being recorded in his Office, was ordered to be recorded Teste JOHN NICHOLAS, C. A. C.

p. [On margin: HILL to GILLASPY, Deed]
418 THIS INDENTURE made this 29th day of June in the year of our Lord one thousand seven hundred and ninety five; Between RICHARD HILL, JUNR. and SALLY his Wife of Albemarle County of the one part and DAVID GILLASPY JUNR. of the said County of the other part; Witnesseth that RICHARD HILL, JUNR. and SALLY his Wife in consideration of the sum of ten pounds current money of Virginia to them in hand paid, do bargain and sell unto DAVID GILLASPY, JUNR. and his heirs one parcel of land in the County of Albemarle containing by estimation sixty one and an half acres be the same more or less and bounded; Begining at a white Oak corner to Doctor THOMAS WALKER and ALEXANDER GILLASPY, thence North forty four degrees West one hundred and eighteen poles to a Chesnut Oak in ALEXANDER GILLASPY's line, North sixty four dgrees East one hundred and nineteen poles to two Chesnut Oaks and a white Oak on the spur of a small Mountain, South forty one degrees East fifty nine poles to two Hickorys and Spanish Oak pointers in the said GILLASPY's line, from thence to the first station; together with all its appurtenances, To have and to hold the parcel of land with appurtenances unto DAVID GILLASPY, JUNR. and his heirs and RICHARD HILL, JUNR. and SALLY his Wife and their heirs the parcel of land with its appurtenances unto DAVID GILLASPY JUNR. and his heirs against all persons will forever warrant and defend, In witness whereof RICHARD HILL, JUNR. and his Wife, SALLY, hath hereunto subscribed their names and affixed their seals on the day and year above written
Signed sealed and delivered in the presence of

[no witnesses recorded] RICHARD HILL
SALLY her mark ✝ HILL

At Albemarle July Court 1795
This Indenture was produced into Court and acknowledged by RICHARD HILL, JUNR. and SALLY his Wife, she being first privately examined as the Law directs, and ordered to be recorded
Teste JOHN NICHOLAS, C. A. C.

pp. [On margin: GILLASPY to GILLASPY, Deed]
418- THIS INDENTURE made this 29th day of June in the year of our Lord one
419 thousand seven hundred and ninety five; Between ALEXANDER GILLASPY and LUCY his Wife of Albemarle County of the one part and DAVID GILLASPY, JUNR. of said County of the other part; Witnesseth that ALEXANDER GILLASPY and his Wife, LUCY, in consideration of the sum of five shillings current money of Virginia to us in hand paid do bargain and sell unto DAVID GILLASPY, JUNR. and his heirs one parcel of land in the County of Albemarle containing by estimation sixty five acres be the same more or less and bounded, Begining at a Hiccory in Doctor THOMAS WALKER's line, thence North fifty five degrees East eighty two poles to a white Oak on the side of the Mountain, North twenty five degrees West seventy five poles to a red Oak and Dogwood near the foot of the Mountain, South forty five degrees East seventy six poles to a white Oak corner to THOMAS WALKER, South forty five degrees West one hundred and fifty poles to a white Oak Stump near to the said WALKER, from thence to the first station together with all its appurtenances, To have and to hold the parcel of land with appurtenances unto DAVID GILLASPY, JUNR. and his heirs and ALEXANDER GILLASPY and LUCY his Wife for themselves and their heirs doth covenant with DAVID GILLASPY, JUNR his heirs the parcel of land with its appurtenances against the claim of every person will warrant and forever defend. In Witness whereof ALEXANDER GILLASPY and LUCY his Wife hath hereunto subscribed their names and affixed their seals the day and year above written
Signed sealed and delivered in presence of
[no witnesses recorded]
ALEXANDER GILLASPY
LUCY her mark ⟨ GILLASPY

At Albemarle July Court 1795
This Indenture was produced into Court and acknowledged by ALEXANDER GILLASPY and LUCY his Wife, she being first privately examined as the Law directs, and ordered to be recorded
Teste JOHN NICHOLAS, C. A. C.

pp. [On margin: GILLASPY to GILLASPY, Deed]
419- THIS INDENTURE made the 29th day of June in the year of our Lord one
420 thousand seven hundred and ninety five; Between ALEXANDER GILLASPY and LUCY his Wife of County of Albemarle of one part and NATHAN GILLASPY of the said County of the other part; Witnesseth that ALEXANDER GILLASPY and LUCY his Wife in consideration of the sum of five shillings current money of Virginia to them in hand paid do bargain and sell unto NATHAN GILLASPY his heirs one parcel of land in the County of Albemarle containing by estimation ninety acres and bounded, Begining at a white Oak in the hollow of a Mountain, thence North sixty five degrees East one hundred and sixty eight poles to a Chesnut

Oak corner to RICHARD HILL, South sixty three degrees East seventy four poles to a red Oak and Dogwood, North twenty five degrees West seventy poles to a white Oak, North fifty five degrees West eighty two poles to a Hiccory, from thence to the first station together with all its appurtenances; To have and to hold the parcel of land with its appurtenances unto NATHAN GILLASPY and his heirs and ALEXANDER GILLASPY and LUCY his Wife do covenant with NATHAN GILLASPY and his heirs against all persons will warrant and defend; In Witness whereof ALEXANDER GILLASPY and his Wife, LUCY, hath hereunto set their hands and seals the day and year above written

Signed sealed and delivered in presence of

[no witnesses recorded] ALEXANDER his mark R GILLASPY
LUCY her mark + GILLASPY

At a Court held for Albemarle County in July 1795
This Indenture was produced into Court and acknowledged by ALEXANDER GILLASPY and LUCY his Wife, she being first privately examined as the Law directs, and ordered to be recorded

Teste JOHN NICHOLAS, C. A. C.

pp. [On margin: BRUMFIELD to CROIT, Deed]
420- THIS INDENTURE made this twenty eighth day of January one thousand
421 seven hundred and ninety five; Between JOHN BRUMFIELD and his Wife, ANNA CHRISTIAN BRUMFIELD, of the one part and JACOB CROIT of the other part [both of Albemarle County] Witnesseth that JOHN BRUMFIELD in consdieration of the sum of one hundred pounds current money of Virginia in hand paid by JACOB CROIT, the receipt whereof they do hereby acknowledge, hath bargained and sold unto JACOB CROIT his heirs one certain tract of land containing one hundred acres more or less lying in County of Albemarle on the waters of SPRING CREEK and bounded; Begining WOOD's and MAUPIN's corner pointers runing thence North forty one and a half degrees East one hundred and forty eight poles to CLARKSON's corner pointers on WOLF PIT BRANCH, then on CLARKSON's line down the Branch South fifty six and a half degrees East one hundred and twenty four poles to a corner red Oak in CLARKSON's line, thence new line South forty one and a half degrees West one hundred and fifty five poles to corner pointers in WOOD's line, then North fifty one degrees West one hundred and twenty four poles to the begining; To have and to hold the tract of land with all appurtenances unto JACOB CROIT his heirs and JOHN BRUMFIELD will warrant and for ever defend the land and premises to JACOB CROIT his heirs against all persons; In Witness whereof JOHN BRUMFIELD and ANNA CHRISTIAN BRUMFIELD his Wife have hereunto set their hands and affixed their seals the day and year above written

Signed sealed and delivered in the presence of

JOHN TAYLOR, JOHN BRUMFIELD
BARTLET GARRETT ANNA CHRISTIAN BRUMFIELD
GEORGE WEST

At Albemarle July Court 1795
This Indenture was produced into Court and acknowledged by JOHN BRUMFIELD, one of the parties thereto, and proved by the Oaths of JOHN TAYLOR, BARTLETT GARRETT and GEORGE WEST, witnesses thereto, as to the Execution by ANNA

CHRISTIAN BRUMFIELD and ordered to be recorded
Teste JOHN NICHOLAS, C. A. C.

pp. [On margin: WALKER to LINDSAY, Deed]
421- TO ALL TO WHOM these presents may come, Know ye that whereas Doctor
422 THOMAS WALKER, deceased, did some years ago deliver REUBIN LINDSAY sundry Negro slaves named Grace, Milley, Little Grace, Jacob, Pheby, Hezekiah, Flora, Edy, George, Mick, Nell and James, which slaves THOMAS WALKER charged REUBIN LINDSAY in account on THOMAS WALKER's Books at fixed prices for each of the slaves with averaging of other charges, I FRANCIS WALKER do by these presents declare that the Account to be fully ballanced and THOMAS WALKER's Books by a Credit which THOMAS WALKER gave REUBIN LINDSAY of one thousand pounds current money as his Wife's fortune above the sum of one hundred pounds which the said WALKER allowed said LINDSAY for his services; Be it Known that I FRANCIS WALKER, Son and Residuary Legatee of THOMAS WALKER, for myself and my heirs do by these presents declare that the right title and interest in the slaves with their present increase is in REUBIN LINDSAY and his heirs and FRANCIS WALKER for himself and his heirs doth by these presents disclaim any right title or interest in the slave their present or future increase. In Witness whereof FRANCIS WALKER hath hereunto subscribed his name and affixed his seal the 15th day of May in the year of our Lord one thousand seven hundred and ninety five
Signed sealed and delivered in the presenceof
THOMAS BIBB, FRANCIS WALKER
JOHN THOMAS,
PETER CLARKSON
At Albemarle July Court 1795
This Release was produced into court and acknowledged by FRANCIS WALKER, party thereto, and ordered to be recorded
Teste JOHN NICHOLAS, C. A. C.

pp. [On margin: JORDAN to HARRIS, Deed]
422- THIS INDENTURE made this twentieth day of June in the year of our Lord
423 one thousand seven hundred and ninety five; Between BENJAMIN JORDAN of BUCKINGHAM County of the one part and MATTHEW HARRIS of AMHERST County of the other part; Witnesseth that BENJAMIN JORDAN in consideration of the sum of five shillings in hand paid, the receipt whereof is hereby acknowledged, hath and by these presents doth bargain and sell unto MATTHEW HARRIS and his heirs one certain tract of land lying in Albemarle County containing one hundred and eight acres being part of a larger tract belonging to the Estate of HOLDER and bound, Begining at pointers on THOMAS's line and runing thence North twenty seven degrees West thirty nine poles to pointers, North thirty four degrees East one hundred and thirty one poles to a corner red Oak, South twenty five and a half degrees East two hundred and fourteen poles to a black Oak in THOMAS's line, South eighty nine degrees West one hundred and twelve poles to the begining; To have and to hold the land and premises with all the appurtenances unto MATTHEW HARRIS his heirs and BENJAMIN JORDAN for himself and his heirs against the

claim of any person will warrant and defend; In Witness whereof BENJAMIN JORDAN hath hereunto set his hand and affixed his seal the day and year first written
Signed sealed and delivered in the presence of
[no witnesses recorded] BENJAMIN JORDAN
At Albemarle July Court 1795
This Indenture was produced into Court and acknowledged by BENJAMIN JORDAN, party thereto, and ordered to be recorded
Teste JOHN NICHOLAS, C. A. C.

pp. [On margin: JORDAN to ELSOM, Deed]
423- THIS INDENTURE made this twentieth day of June in the year of our Lord
424 one thousand seven hundred and ninety five; Between BENJAMIN JORDAN of BUCKINGHAM County of the one part and WILLIAM ELSOM of Albemarle County of the other part; Witnesseth that BENJAMIN JORDAN in consideration of the sum of five shillings to him in hand paid the receipt whereof he doth hereby acknowledge, hath and by these presents doth bargain and sell unto WILLIAM ELSOM his heirs one certain tract of land lying in the County of Albemarle on HOG CREEK being the same BENJAMIN JORDAN purchased at a Sheriff's Sale for taxes due thereon containing one hundred and three acres be the same more or less and bounded, Begining at a Chesnut corner on NICHOLAS's line and runing thence North eighty seven degrees West thirty poles to a Hiccory and white Oak, South twenty seven degrees West to a corner in the Old Field, South twenty one degrees West eighty eight poles to pointers on bushes, South twenty five degrees East one hundred and seven poles to a scrub Oak, North twenty four degrees East one hundred and forty four poles to pointers, thence South fifty degrees West seventy six poles to the begining; To have and to hold the tract of land and all and singular the appurtenances unto WILLIAM ELSOM and his heirs and BENJAMIN JORDAN for himself and his heirs against the claim of every person will warrant and defend; In Witness whereof BENJAMIN JORDAN hath hereunto set his hand and affixed his seal the day and year first written
Signed sealed and delivered in the presence of
JOHN LEWIS, JUNR. BENJAMIN JORDAN
CLOUGH SHELTON,
JOHN STEELE,
RICHARD BARBOUR
At Albemarle July Court 1795
This Indenture was produced into Court and acknowledged by BENJAMIN JORDAN, party thereto, and ordered to be recorded
Teste JOHN NICHOLAS C. A. C.

pp. [On margin: FITZGERRALD to WOOD, Deed.. Delivered to JAMES WOOD
424- 22d of August 1839]
425 THIS INDENTURE made this sixth day of July in the year of our Lord one thousand seven hundred and ninety five, Between BARTLETT FITZGERRALD and MASK his Wife of the County of Albemarle of one part and WILLIAM WOOD of said County of the other part; Witnesseth that in consideration of the sum

of twenty nine pounds, sixteen shillings and nine pence BARTLETT FITZGERRALD and MASK his Wife hath bargained and sold unto WILLIAM WOOD one certain tract of land lying in County of Albemarle on the Branches of BEAVER CREEK and containing eighty five and a quarter acres and bounded; Begining at a black Gum in ARCHIBALD WOOD's line, thence North sixteen degrees East one hundred and seventy poles to a Poast Oak in DAVID MILLS's Old Line, thence with MILLS's line South seventy degrees East sixty seven poles to a Pine Stump in a Path corner to said MILLS, South eighty one degrees East thirty one poles to a Pine and white Oak saplins pointers in the head of a hollow, South four degrees East forty four poles to a stone in WILLIAM WOOD's Field, then with the said WOOD's line South eighty eight degrees West nineteen poles to a lying down Pine, then South forty one degrees West one hundred and fifty three poles to a white Oak Stump corner to WILLIAM WOOD's in ARCHIBALD WOOD's Old Line, then with his line North fifty degrees West thirty two poles to the begining; To have and to hold the eighty five and a quarter acres of land with its appurtenances unto WILLIAM WOOD his heirs and BARTLETT GERRALD and MASK his Wife for themselves and their heirs doth by these presents forever warrant and defend the land with appurtenances unto WILLIAM WOOD his heirs against the claim and demand of any person; In Witness whereof BARTLETT GERRALD and MASK his Wife hath hereunto set their hands and affixed their seals the day and year above mentioned
In presence of
[no witnesses recorded] BARTLET FITZGERRALD
MASKIE her mark GERRALD

At Albemarle July Court 1795
This Indenture was produced into Court and acknowledged by BARTLETT FITZGARRALD and MASKIE his Wife, she being first privately examined as the Law directs, and ordered to be recorded
Teste JOHN NICHOLAS, C. A. C.

pp. [On margin: JARMAN to MAUPIN, Deed]
425- THIS INDENTURE made this fourth day of July in the year of our Lord one
426 thousand seven hundred and ninety five; Between WILLIAM JARMAN of Albemarle County of one part and DANIEL MAUPIN of said County of other part; Witnesseth that WILLIAM JARMAN in consideration of the sum of thirty pounds Virginia currency to him in hand paid by DANIEL MAUPIN the receipt whereof he doth hereby confess and acknowledge, hath and by these presents doth bargain and sell unto DANIEL MAUPIN and to his heirs one certain tract of land containing by estimation forty acres more of less bounded being in Albemarle County, Begining on DOYLES RIVER where MAXARY EWELL's line crosses, thence on MAXCEY EWELL's line South sixty five degrees West to JOHN MAUPIN's line, thence on JOHN MAUPIN's line the same course to MOREMAN's RIVER, thence down the River to the mouth of DOYLES RIVER, thence up DOYLES RIVER to the first station, together with all improvements and appurtenancs to the tract of land belonging To have and to hold the tract of land with all improvements thereto being unto DANIEL MAUPIN his heirs and WILLIAM JARMAN for himself and his heirs the tract of land unto DANEIL MAUPIN his heirs will hereafter warrant and defend a good and perfect estate of inheritance in fee simple to DANIEL MAUPIN his heirs,

In Witness whereof WILLIAM JARMAN hath hereunto set his hand and seal this day first above written
Signed sealed and delivered in presence of
[no witnesses recorded] WILLIAM JARMAN
At Albemarle July Court 1795
This Indenture was produced into Court and acknowledged by WILLIAM JARMAN, party thereto, and ordered to be recorded
Teste JOHN NICHOLAS, C. A. C.

p. [On margin: ANDERSON to COLES Deed]
426 KNOW ALL MEN by these presents that I GEORGE ANDERSON of the County of CUMBERLAND in consideration of the sum of seventy pounds to me in hand paid by JOHN COLES of the County of Albemarle, the receipt whereof I do hereby acknowledge, have bargained and sold unto JOHN COLES his heirs a Negro man slave named James and I do hereby for the consideration aforesaid warrant and defend the title property and posession of the Negro man, James, unto JOHN COLES his heirs against the title claim or demand of all persons claiming from me the said GEORGE ANDERSON, In Witness whereof I have hereunto set my hand and affixed my seal this twenty ninth day of September in the year of our Lord one thousand seven hundred and ninety four
Signed sealed and delivered in the presence of
SAMUEL DYER, GEORGE ANDERSON
CHRISTOPHER HUDSON
At Albemarle July Court 1795
This Bill of Sale was produced into Court and proved by the Oaths of SAMUEL DYER and CHRISTOPHER HUDSON, witnesses thereto, and ordered to be recorded
Teste JOHN NICHOLAS, C. A. C.

pp,. [On margin: BROWN to BROWN, Deed]
426- THIS INDENTURE made this twentieth day of April in the year of our Lord
427 one thousand seven hundred and ninety five; Between BENAJAH BROWN of one part of Albemarle County and BERNARD BROWN of said County of other part; Witnesseth that BENAJAH BROWN and MARY his Wife in consideration of the sum of four hundred and sixty pounds to them in cash in hand paid the receipt whereof they do hereby acknowledge hath bargained and sold unto BERNARD BROWN his heirs one certain tract of land lying in County of Albemarle whereon the said BENAJAH BROWN now lives and bounded; Begining at pointers at the upper corner of the Branch, down the same with its meanders to a red Oak and Chesnut, thence North eighty six degrees East one hundred and six poles to a corner Poplar in a valley, thence South fifteen degrees East one hundred and ninety two poles to a dead Lynn on said Branch, thence South eighty six degrees West four hundred and ten poles to pointers and a Rock, thence North eleven degrees East seventeen poles to pointers, thence North eighty eight degrees West sixty four poles to a black Gum in a dry Branch, North nine and one half degrees West ninety one poles to a Chesnut Oak, North eighty two degrees West twenty four poles to pointers, South twenty four degrees West thirty four poles to a Chesnut Oak in a valley, South eighty three degrees West fifty poles to a Chesnut North forty five degrees West one hundred and seven

poles to a forked Chesnut, South sixty one degrees West sixty poles to a Chesnut Oak on a Hill side, South fifteen degrees East forty poles to a Spanish Oak and Hiccory, North fourteen degrees, West sixty eight poles to a Chesnut Oak on the top of the Mountain, North thirty degrees East thirty seven poles to lpointers, South sixty eight degrees East fifteen poles to a large Chesnut, North forty seven degrees East eighty eight poles to a Spanish Oak, North eighty two degrees East fifty six poles to pointers of Gums North forty six degrees East twenty eight poles to pointers, South seventy three degrees East fifty four poles to pointers [saplins] North seventy five degrees East fifty poles to a Hiccory, North fourteen degrees East twenty five poles to a Chesnut, North eighty degrees East thirteen poles to pointers, North eleven and one half degrees East sixty five poles to a white Oak, North thirty eight degrees East eighteen poles and containing seven hundred and eighty six acres unto BERNARD BROWN and his heirs free from the claim of BENAJAH BROWN and MARY his Wife their heirs and BENAJAH BROWN and MARY his Wife will warrant and defend the land and appurtenances unto BERNARD BROWN his heirs, In Witness whereof we have hereunto set our hands and seals the day and date above written

Signed sealed and delivered in the presence of

BERNIS BROWN, BENAJAH BROWN
BAZELEEL BROWN, MARY BROWN
BRIGHTBERRY BROWN

At Albemarle July Court 1795

This Indenture was produced into Court and acknowledged by BENAJAH BROWN, one of the parties thereto, and ordered to be recorded

Teste JOHN NICHOLAS, C. A. C.

p. [On margin: CARRs Exrs. to TERREL, Deed. Delivered to C. TERREL]

428 THIS INDENTURE made this sixth day of July in the year of our Lord one thousand seven hundred and ninety five; Between THOMAS CARR, GARLAND CARR and NATHANIEL ANDERSON of Albemarle County, Executors of JOHN CARR, deceased, of the one part and CHILES TERRELL of the aforesaid County of the other part; Witnesseth that THOMAS CARR, GARLAND CARR and NATHANIEL ANDERSON in consideration of the sum of two hundred and fifty pounds current money of Virginia to them in hand paid by CHILES TERRELL, the receipt whereof they do hereby acknowledge, hath and by these presents doth bargain and sell unto CHILES TERRELL his heirs one certain tract of land lying in County of Albemarle on the North side of the LITTLE MOUNTAINS containing four hundred and thirty acres more or less and bounded, Begining at three Pines near McCAULEY's Spring South seventy six degrees thirty minutes East one hundred and twenty poles to a Pine, South sixty six degrees thirty minutes East forty one poles to two Pines, South twenty seven degrees East sixty four poles to several marked trees near the Creek, North eighty six and one half degrees East three hundred and forty poles to several trees in the head of a bottom, North forty one and one half degrees West three hundred and twenty poles to three Pines, South sixty two degrees West three hundred and forty eight poles to the begining adjoining the lands of GEORGE TAYLOR, DANIEL FERGERSON, JAMES SEBREE, JOHN DOWELL, JUNR. JOHN DOWELL, SENR. and JOHN McCAULEY, together with all and singular the appurtenances thereunto belonging, To have and to hold the the tract of land and

premises with the appurtenances unto CHILES TERRELL his heirs and THOMAS CARR, GARLAND CARR and NATHANIEL ANDERSON, Executors as aforesaid, unto CHILES TERRELL his heirs against the claim and demand of any person will warrant and forever defend by these prsents; In Testimony whereof they have hereunto set their hands and affixed their seals the day and year first above written
Signed sealed and delivered in presence of

[no witnesses recorded] THOMAS CARR
GARLAND CARR
NATHANIEL ANDERSON

At Albemarle July Court 1795
This Indenture was produced into Court and acknowledged by THOMAS CARR, GARLAND CARR and NATHANIEL ANDERSON, Executors of JOHN CARR, deceased, and ordered to be recorded
Teste JOHN NICHOLAS, C A. C.

p. [On margin; HUDSON to HUDSON, Deed]
429 KNOW ALL MEN by these presents that I CHRISTOPHER HUDSON as Trustee for a Debt due by CHARLES HUDSON to Messrs. COCKRAN and DAVISON, Merchants at SCOTT's FERRY in Albemarle County, being called upon by Messrs. COCKRAN and DAVISON to carry into effect the Deed of Trust have set up the following slaves being those made over to me in Trust to satisfy the Debt to Messrs. COCKRAN and DAVISON, to wit, Melatto Robin, Lewis Son of Lewis and Hannah, which slaves were sold to MARTHA EPPES HUDSON for thirty five pounds current money of Virginia the receipt whereof I do hereby acknowledge, and I do [as Trustee aforesaid] deliver and convey unto MARTHA EPPES HUDSON and to her heirs the right title interest claim and demand I or my heirs may have in the aforesaid slaves and their future increase and I do hereby warrant and forever defend the aforesaid slaves from myself my heirs; In Witness whereof I have hereunto set my hand and affixed my seal this [blank] day of [blank] one thousand seven hundred and ninety five
Signed sealed and delivered in the presence of

[no witnesses recorded] CHRISTOPHER HUDSON

At Albemarle July Court 1795
This Deed Poll was produced into Court and acknowledged by CHRISTOPHER HUDSON, party thereto and ordered to be recorded
Teste JOHN CARR, Dep. Cl.

pp. [On margin: WALKER & Ux to JONES, Commission]
429- The Commonwealth of Virginia to WILSON CARY NICHOLAS and
430 CHARLES WINGFIELD, JUNR. Gentlemen Greeting. Whereas WILLIAM WALKER and ELIZABETH his Wife by their certain Indenture of bargain and sale bearing date the nineteenth day of May 1795 have conveyed unto LAIN JONES one certain tract of land lying in County of Albemarle and containing by estimation four hundred acres and whereas ELIZABETH cannot conveniently travel to our County Court of Albemarle to make acknowledgment of the conveyance [the Commission for taking the acknowledgment and privy examination of ELIZABETH, Wife of WILLIAM WALKER] Witness JOHN NICHOLAS, Clerk of our said Court, he 2d day of June 1795 and in the 19th year of our Foundation JOHN NICHOLAS, C. A. C.

By virtue of the within Commisson we examined ELIZABETH WALKER privily and apart from her Husband, WILLIAM WALKER, who declared she acknowledged the annexed Deed willingly and freely without the threats of WILLIAM WALKER her Husband and that she is willing the same shall be recorded in the County Court of Albemarle Witness our hands and seals this Eleventh day of June 1795

WILSON CARY NICHOLAS
CHARLES WINGFIELD, JUNR.

At Albemarle July Court 1795
This Commission and Certificate of the Relinquishment of ELIZABETH WALKER's Dower in a certain tract of land conveyed by WILLIAM WALKER, her Husband, to LAIN JONES, was returned and ordered to be recorded

Teste JOHN CARR, Dep Cl

pp. [On margin: KEY to Governor Sheriff's Bond]
430- KNOW ALL MEN by these presents that we JOHN KEY, PETER CLARK-
431 SON, DAVID CLARKSON, JOSHUA KEY, AMBROSE EDWARDS and GRAVIT EDWARDS are held and firmly bound unto ROBERT BROOK, Governor or Chief Magistrate of the Commonwealth of Virginia for the time being and his successors for the use of the Commonwealth in the sum of thirty thousand Dollars to be paid to ROBERT BROOK and his successors in Office for the time being for the use of the Commonwealth, to which payment well and truly to be made we and each of us by these presents jointly and severally bind ourselves our heirs firmly by these presents, Sealed with our seals and dated this 3d day of August 1795

THE CONDITION of the above Obligation is such that whereas the above bound JOHN KEY is constituted and appointed Sheriff of the County of Albemarle by a Commission from the Governor under the Seal of the Commonwealth dated the eighteenth day of June last past, If therefore JOHN KEY do well and truly collect and receive all taxes becoming due within the County and pay the same to the Treasurer of the Commonwealth for the time being for the use of the Commnwealth within the time prescribed and limited by Law and shall in all things truly and faithfully execute the Office of Sheriff during his continuance therein, then the above Obligation to be void, otherwise to remain in full force and virtue

Signed sealed and delivered in open Court JOHN KEY
PETER CLARKSON
DAVID CLARKSON
AMBROSE EDWARDS
GRAVIT EDWARDS
JOSHUA KEY

pp. [On margin: KEY to Governor, Sheriff's Bond]
431- KNOW ALL MEN by these presents that we JOHN KEY, PETER CLARK-
432 SON, DAVID CLARKSON, AMBROSE EDWARDS, GRAVIT EDWARDS and JOSHUA KEY are held and firmly bound unto ROBERT BROOKE, Governor or Chief Magistrate of the Commonwealth of Virginia for the time being and his successors for the use of the Commnwealth in the sum of thirty thousand Dollars to be paid to ROBERT BROOK and his successors in Office to which payment well and truly to be made we and each of us do jointly and severally bind ourselves our

heirs firmly by these presents, Sealed with our seals and dated this 3d day of August 1795

THE CONDITION of the above Obligation is such that whereas the above bound JOHN KEY is constituted and appointed Sheriff of the County of Albemarle by a Commission from the Governor under the seal of the Commonwealth dated the eighteenth day of June last past, If JOHN KEY shall well and truly collect all levies and account for and pay the same in such manner as is by Law directed and also all fines, forfeitures and amercements accruing and becoming due to the Treasurer of the Commonwealth in like manner as is or shall be directed in case of publick Taxes and shall in all other things truly and faithfully execute the Office of Sheriff during his continuance therein, then the above Obligaton to be void otherwise to remain in full force and virtue

Signed sealed and delivered in open Court JOHN KEY
PETER CLARKSON
DAVID CLARKSON
AMBROSE EDWARDS
GRAVIT EDWARDS
JOSHUA KEY

pp. [On margin: KEY to Governor, Sheriff's Bond]
432- KNOW ALL MEN by these presents that we JOHN KEY, PETER CLARK-
433 SON, DAVID CLARKSON, AMBROSE EDWARDS, GRAVIT EDWARDS and JOSHUA KEY are held and firmly bound unto ROBERT BROOK, Governor or Chief Magistrate of the Commonwealth of Virginia for the time being and his successors for the use of the Commonwealth in the sum of thirty thousand Dollars to be paid to ROBERT BROOK and his successors in Office for the time being, to which payment well and truly to be made we bind ourselves our heirs jointly and severally firmly by these presents, Sealed with our seals and dated this 3d day of August 1795

THE CONDITION of the above Obligation is such that whereas the above bound JOHN KEY is constituted and appointed Sheriff of the County of Albemarle by Commission from the Governor under the Seal of the Commonwealth dated the eighteenth day of June last past, If JOHN KEY shall well and truly collect and receive all offices fees and dues put into his hands to collect and duly account for and pay the same to the Officers to whom such fees are due respectively at such times as are prescribed and limited by Law, and shall well and truly execute and due return make of all Process and Precepts to him directed, and pay and satisfy all sums of money by him received by virtue of any such Process to the person or persons to whom the same is due, and in all other things shall truly and faithfully executed and perform the Office of Sheriff during the time of his continuance therein, then the above Obligation to be void, otherwise to remain in full force and virtue

Signed sealed and delivered in open Court JOHN KEY
PETER CLARKSON
DAVID CLARKSON
AMBROSE EDWARDS
GRAVIT EDWARDS
JOSHUA KEY

pp. [On margin: HOPKINS to NICHOLAS, Deed, 500 acres]
433- THIS INDENTURE made this first day of April in the year of our Lord one
435 thousand seven hundred and ninety five; Between JAMES HOPKINS and ANN S. HOPKINS his Wife of the County of AMHERST of the one part and JOHN NICHOLAS of Albemarle County of the other part; Witnesseth that in consideration of the sum of four hundred pounds to JAMES HOPKINS in hand paid, the receipt whereof he doth hereby acknowledge, hath and by these presents doth bargain and sell unto JOHN NICHOLAS his heirs one certain tract of land lying in the County of Albemarle and FLUVANNA near SCOTT's FERRY on JAMES RIVER containing by three several surveys five hundred acres and bounded as expressed in two certain Patents one bearing date the 27th day of August 1783, the other the 16th day of March 1792, now of Record in the Register's Office of this State also a Deed from WILLIAM HOPKINS and MARY his Wife dated the 2d day of December 1784, now of Record in the County of Albemarle, all made and rendered unto JAMES HOPKINS from which first mentioned Patent which contains four hundred acres is excluded and reserved from this Deed seventy nine acres for the further use and possession of JAMES HOPKINS on the Northwest corner of the above mentioned survey and parcels of land adjoining the lands of WILLIAM HOPKINS and WILLIAM HAMNER so as to reduce the several surveys contained in the Patents and Deeds to five hundred acres, which five hundred acres is bounded, Begining at pointers and runing North thirteen degrees West seventy poles to pointers, North thirty three degees West forty six poles to pointers on JOPLINs ROAD, then leaving the Road agreeable to its course North forty eight degrees East eighteen poles North forty degrees East twenty two poles, then leaving the Road eight poles same course to the Road, then along the same North thirty six degrees East twelve poles to the mouth of MOORE's ROAD, then with the same North twenty seven degrees thirty minutes East sixteen poles to pointers on the East side of the Road, thence along the same North four degrees West twelve poles, North five degrees East thirty four poles to pointers on the Road, then leaving the Road North eighty eight degrees East one hundred and twelve poles to a Pine, South five degrees East twenty six poles to pointers, North three degrees West two hundred twenty nine poles to pointers, North twenty five degrees East two hundred twenty two poles to two Pines, South four degrees East one hundred and ninety five poles to a Pine, then South fifty degrees East one hundred and sixty eight poles to pointers by the Path, thence up the Path according to its meanders one hundred twenty five poles to a Pine, South forty one and an half degrees East one hundred and thirty four poles to a Pine, North sixty one and an half degrees West seventy nine poles to pointers, South twenty seven degrees West one hundred thirty six poles to pointers, South sixty one degrees West forty seven poles to the first station together with all and singular the appurtenances thereunto belonging To have and to hold the parcel of land of five hundred acres and premises with the appurtenances thereunto belonging unto JOHN NICHOLAS his heirs and JAMES HOPKINS and ANN SPARKS his Wife doth hereby covenant and agree to and with JOHN NICHOLAS that they will warrant and defend the title in fee simple of the parcel of land against the claim of all persons; In Witness whereof JAMES HOPKINS and ANNE SPARKS his Wife have hereunto set their hands and affixed their seals the day and year before written

Signed sealed and delivered in presence of
HENRY MARTIN, SENR. JAMES HOPKINS
LEWIS NICHOLAS ANNE S. HOPKINS
JOHN GRIFF

Albemarle County Sct. The Commonwealth of Virginia to JOHN DIGGS, WILLIAM HARRIS and JOSEPH SHELTON, Gentlemen, Greeting. Whereas JAMES HOPKINS and ANNE SPARKS his Wife have by their Indenture of bargain and sale bearing date the 1st day of April 1795, bargained and sold unto JOHN NICHOLAS one certain tract of land lying in County of Albemarle near SCOTT's FERRY on JAMES RIVER containing five hundred acres, and whereas it appears that ANNE SPARKS cannot conveniently travel to our County Court of Albemarle to make acknowledgment of the Indenture, [the Commission for taking the acknowledgment and privy examination of ANNE SPARKS, Wife of JAMES HOPKINS] Witness JOHN NICHOLAS Clerk of our said Court the first day of April 1795 and in the 19th year of our Foundation

JOHN NICHOLAS, C. A. C.

Pursuant to the above Commission to us directed we proceeded to examine ANNE SPARKS HOPKINS therein mentioned seperate and apart from her Husband, [the return of the execution of the privy examination of ANNE SPARKS HOPKINS] Given under our hands and seals this 7th day of May 1795

WILLIAM HARRIS
JOSEPH SHELTON

At Albemarle September Court 1795
This Indenture, Commisson and Certificate for the Relinquishment of ANNE SPARKS HOPKINS's Dower in a certain tract of land conveyed by JAMES HOPKINS her Husband to JOHN NICHOLAS was produced into Court and ordered to be recorded being first acknowledged by JAMES HOPKINS party thereto

Teste JOHN CARR, Dep. Cl

[Albemarle County Deed Book No 11, 1793-1795, will continue in another book begining on page 436 with the Deed from OLIVER TOWLES to REUBIN RUCKER and JOHN TERRELL JUNR.]

www.ingramcontent.com/pod-product-compliance
Lightning Source LLC
LaVergne TN
LVHW061249100826
845148LV00008B/1070
* 9 7 8 1 6 8 0 3 4 2 5 9 8 *